Since the pages of this book was digitalized from a very old original, the pages here may look a little funny at times. Rest assured we did our best to format the original book into modern form as best allowed by the current processes available.

Although each page of this book was copied from the original edition, this reprint is in no way endorsed by or associated with the original author Harry Johnson.

Ross Brown

Introduction and Cover Art Copyright 2008 -
All rights reserved.
TheDesignHouse
ISBN 1440454418

For regular updates on new reprint editions of
vinatge cocktail books,
vintage wine books,
vintage drinks books and
vintage cooking books
please visit

www.VintageCocktailBooks.com

Harry Johnson, the "DEAN" of Bartenders, published this original manual about 1860. This complete guide for mixing drinks and running a successful bar was the authoritative manual when drinking was an art. The prices shown in this revised edition are Harry's own—out of date to be sure—the recipes, however, we vouch for. Some brands mentioned are now not obtainable—substitute modern brands.

THE PUBLISHER.

THE NEW AND IMPROVED

ILLUSTRATED

BARTENDERS' MANUAL

OR:

HOW TO MIX DRINKS

OF THE

PRESENT STYLE,

Containing Valuable Instructions and Hints by the Author in Reference to the Management of a Bar, a Hotel and a Restaurant; also a Large List of Mixed Drinks, including American, British, French, German, Italian, Russian, Spanish, etc., with Illustrations and a Comprehensive Description of Bar Utensils, Wines, Liquors, Ales, Mixtures, etc., etc.

1934

REVISED EDITION.

CHARLES E. GRAHAM & CO.
NEWARK, N. J.
MADE IN U. S. A.

PREFACE BY THE AUTHOR

In submitting this manual to the public, I crave indulgence for making a few remarks in regard to myself.

The profession—for such it must be admitted—of mixing drinks was learned by me, in San Francisco, and, since then, I have had forty years' experience. Leaving California, in 1868, I opened, in Chicago, what was generally recognized to be the largest and finest establishment of the kind in this country. But the conflagration of 1871 caused me a loss of $100,000 and, financially ruined, I was compelled to start life anew. It was at this time that I was taught the value of true friendship, for numerous acquaintances tendered me material assistance, which was, however, gratefully declined.

Though later engaged in Boston, at a leading hotel, I soon returned to New York and was employed in one of the well-known hostelries of the Metropolis until enabled to begin a business of my own, which has since been pre-eminently successful.

There was published by me, in San Francisco, the first Bartender's Manual ever issued in the United States. This publication was a virtual necessity—the result of a constant demand for such a treatise by those everywhere engaged in the hotel, bar and restaurant business. As a proof, ten thousand (10,000) copies of the work were sold at a price much larger than the present cost within the brief period of six weeks.

In 1869, I was challenged by five of the most popular and scientific bartenders of the day to engage in a tourney of skill, at New Orleans, with the sequence that to me was awarded the championship of the United States.

To recapitulate:—Having been in the hotel and liquor business, in various capacities, since my boyhood, being employed in some of the most prominent hotels, restaurants, and cafés of several large cities, and having traveled extensively in this and other countries—especially of Continental Europe—for the sole purpose of learning the methods of preparing the many different kinds of mixed drinks, with the highest letters of recommendation acknowledging my thorough ability, I have, after careful preparation with much time and expense, succeeded in compiling this work which is now offered in a revised and up-to-date form. There is described and illustrated, in plain language, the popular mixed concoctions, fancy beverages, cocktails, punches, juleps, etc. This volume also furnishes comprehensive instructions to be observed in attending a bar, in personal conduct, how to serve and wait on customers, and all the various details connected with the business so definitely stated that any person contemplating starting in life as a bartender has a perfect and valuable guide to aid him in a complete mastery of his line of labor. This manual likewise gives a complete list of all bar utensils, glass and silver ware, mixtures, liquors, and different brands of beverages that will be required, with directions for their proper use. There is, additionally, a large number of valuable hints and items of information for bartenders and, in fact, every detail that may be of importance from the moment one steps behind the bar through all the requirements of each day succeeding. Those who are thoroughly experienced, and whose competence has long since been conceded, have also found this work to be of value to them. They have always acknowledged it to be "a handy volume."

The principle I desire to instill is that this vocation —that of eating and drinking—to be properly successful, must be conducted by the same legitimate methods as any other monied enterprise that appeals directly to the public. It furnishes a necessity, just as does the clothier, hatter, and shoe-dealer, and, in itself, is an honorable means of livelihood. It should not be regarded by the proprietor or employee as a special means of securing the patronage of friends, as a possible avenue of good luck, or as a chance to gain by nefarious opportunities. It should be managed alone in an earnest, honorable manner. Believe in yourself, and others will have faith in you.

The writer has also made—for many years past— a profession of teaching the art of attending a bar to any one expressing an inclination to learn. In the great number of those who have received instruction from me in the latest methods and scientific manipulation, I can with pride refer as testimonial of my fitness as a teacher of bartending.

In conclusion, I desire to state that this publication,

in its first edition, was the primary work of the kind in the United States, if not in the world; and that I am the originator of a form of manual instruction that may be classified as a contribution to trade literature. Imitation is always the sincerest form of flattery and, consequently, attempts have been made to furnish the public with similar efforts by others—efforts that have failed to detract from the popularity and efficiency of *Harry Johnson's Bartender's Manual.*

But it is to be noted that this volume is not alone intended as a guide to those serving at the bar. Its purpose is to be a work of reference, as well, for the proprietors of hotels, restaurants, clubs, steamship lines, public dining-rooms, and all those engaged in catering to the general needs of "the inner man."

It is my hope that this guide will not only prove serviceable to the profession, for whom it is specifically intended, but, furthermore, to the family circle and the public in general. The style and art of mixing is indicated in the twenty odd illustrations that are given in the work, special attention being called to plates Nos. 1 and 3. Plate No. 2 is, likewise, pertinent to the text.

Very respectfully yours,

HARRY JOHNSON.

INDEX.

RULES AND REGULATIONS.

FROM 1 TO 56.

	PAGE.
How to attend a bar	21
How a Bartender may obtain a Situation	22
The Mutual Relations of Employer and Employee	24
Rules for Bartenders in entering and going off duty	28
First Duty in opening a Bar-room in the morning	29
Why Bartenders should have their own Union for Protection and Association	33
Getting your Money when busy or in a rush	38
Hints about training a Boy to the business	39
Treatment of Patrons—Behavior towards them	40
How to improve the appearance of Bar and Toilet Rooms	42
To know how a customer desires his drink to be mixed	45
Hints from the Author	45
The Opening of a New Place	49
Having a complete Price-List	52
To keep Ants and other insects out of mixing bottles	53
Handling Champagnes and other wines	54
Cleaning Silverware, Mirrors, etc	54
How Corks should be drawn from wine bottles	58
Glassware for Strained Drinks	59
The Ice Box in your Basement or Cellar	59

	PAGE.
How to handle properly Liquors in casks or bottles..	63
A few remarks about Case Goods.....................	64
A Tip to Beginners—How to make money..........	70
Keeping Books in a simple manner..................	76
A Restaurant in connection with a Cafe.............	78
In connection with the Check System................	94
Concerning High Proof of Liquors..................	99
Some remarks about Mortgages......................	101
A few remarks about Cashing Checks..................	104
Rules in reference to a Gigger.......................	107
A few remarks regarding Lager Beer................	108
How Lager Beer should be drawn and served........	109
About bottled Lager Beer, imported as well as domestic	113
About Cleaning Beer and Ale pipes..................	113
Relating to Punch Bowls............................	114
The proper style of opening and serving Champagne	115
Purchasing Supplies	116
Handing Bar spoons to Customers.....................	118
How to keep a Cellar and Store Room...............	118
How to Clean Brass and other Metals................	122
Keeping Glassware	123
How to handle Ice...................................	127
The purchase of an old Place........................	128
The opening of Mineral Waters......................	132
How Drinks should be served at tables.............	133
How Claret Wines should be handled.................	133
Treatment of Mineral Waters........................	135
In reference to Free Lunch..........................	135
How to handle Ale and Porter in casks...............	137
Cordials, Bitters and Syrups........................	138
How Ale and Porter should be drawn................	139
Decorating Drinks with Fruit........................	140
How to handle Fruits, Eggs and Milk................	140
Concerning Bar Fixtures with Gauze in the summer	143
Cigars sold at bar and elsewhere.....................	144
Last but not Least...................................	146

LIST OF UTENSILS, WINES, LIQUORS AND PRINCIPAL STOCK OF RESTAURANT AND CAFE.

FROM 57 TO 70.

PAGE.

Complete List of Utensils, etc., used in a Bar Room 147
List of Glassware.................................... 149
List of different Liquors............................ 149
List of Wines.. 151
List of Cordials..................................... 151
List of Ales and Porter.............................. 152
List of Mineral Waters............................... 152
List of Principal Syrups............................. 153
List of Principal Bitters............................ 153
List of Principal Fruits used in a Cafe.............. 153
List of Principal Mixtures........................... 154
Sundries 154
The Principal Stock of a Restaurant.................. 154
The Principal Stock of a Cafe........................ 156

LIST OF MIXED DRINKS.

FROM 71 TO 337.

A

PAGE.

Absinthe Cocktail 163
American Style of Mixing Absinthe.................... 176
Apple Jack Sour...................................... 187
Ale Sangaree 199
Arf and Arf.. 203
Absinthe Frappe 245
Apple Jack Cocktail.................................. 256
Apollinaris Lemonade 260
April Shower... 267
American Glory....................................... 267

E

	PAGE.
Egg-Nogg	169
East India Cocktail	187
Empire Punch	194
Egg Lemonade	195
Egg Milk Punch	197
English Bishop	216
English Royal Punch	232
English Curaçoa	233
Egg Sour	249
Eye-Opener	259

F

Fancy Whiskey Smash	170
Fancy Brandy Cocktail	172
Faivre's Pousse Cafe	178
Fancy Brandy Smash	182
Fine Lemonade for Parties	215
Fancy Brandy Sour	231
Fedora	235

G

Golden Slipper	168
German or Swiss Style of Mixing Absinthe	177
Golden Fizz	178
Gin Fizz	186
General Harrison Egg-Nogg	200
Gin and Calamus	211
Gin and Milk	217
Gin and Wormwood	219
Gin Fix	220
Gin and Tansy	224
Gin Julep	225
Gin Cocktail	226
Gin Smash	228

	PAGE.
Gin Toddy	230
Gin and Molasses	231
Gin Sour	240
Gin Rickey	241
Gin Daisy	256
Golden Thistle	264

H

How to Mix Absinthe	176
How to Mix Tom and Jerry	187
How to Deal out Tom and Jerry	188
Hot Spiced Rum	197
Hot Apple Toddy	202
Hot Lemonade	203
How to Serve a Pony Glass of Brandy	218
Hot Gin Sling	218
Hot Arrac Punch	224
Hot Scotch Whiskey Sling	225
Hot Milk Punch	226
Hot Whiskey	227
Hot Locomotive	228
Hot Irish Whiskey Punch	229
Hot Rum	231
Hot Brandy Sling	239
Hot Egg-Nogg	249
Hot Brandy Punch	250
Hot Scotch Whiskey Punch	250
Highball	251
Hot English Rum Punch	252
Horse's Neck	259
High Life	268

I

Italian Style of Mixing Absinthe	177
Imperial Brandy Punch	208
Irish Cocktail	243
Imperial Cocktail	263

J

	PAGE.
Japanese Cocktail	193
John Collins	198
Jersey Cocktail	204
Jamaica Rum Sour	224

K

Knickerbocker	170
Knickebein	180
Kirschwasser Punch	201
Klondyke Cocktail	264

L

Lemonade	191
Little Egypt	268

M

Mint Julep	161
Morning Glory Fizz	162
Manhattan Cocktail	162
Mississippi Punch	166
Milk Punch	179
Medford Rum Sour	184
Maywine Punch	196
Mulled Claret and Egg	201
Milk and Selters	212
Medford Rum Smash	220
Medford Rum Punch	227
Morning Cocktail	242
Maraschino Punch	260
Martini Cocktail	165
Montana Cocktail	261
Marguerite Cocktail	263
Maiden's Dream	264
Morning Daisy	265

O

	PAGE.
Old Style Whiskey Smash	198
Orange Lemonade	204
Orgeat Lemonade	218
Orchard Punch	228
Old Tom Gin Cocktail	230
Orange Punch	236
Old-Fashioned Whiskey Cocktail	242
Old Style American Punch	244
Oyster Cocktail	262
Olivette Cocktail	265

P

Pousse Cafe	160
Pousse L'Amour	165
Port Wine Punch	184
Prussian Grandeur Punch	192
Porter Sangaree	202
Punch à la Ford	216
Port Wine Flip	224
Port Wine Sangaree	239
Port Wine Cobbler	240
Peach and Honey	241
Punch à la Dwyer	243
Philippine Punch	244
Punch à la Romaine	247
Porter Cup for a party	248
Parisian Pousse Cafe	249
Port Wine Lemonade	258

R

Roman Punch	166
Rhine Wine Cobbler	201
Rhine Wine and Selters	208
Raspberry Shrub	210

	PAGE.
Rochester Punch	235
Rock and Rye	240
Remsen Cooler	256
Russian Punch	261
Reform Cocktail	264

S

Sherry Cocktail	248
Snow Ball	257
Saratoga Cooler	259
Silver Fizz	165
Sherry Cobbler	169
Sherry Flip	171
St. Charles Punch	175
Selters Lemonade	180
Sauterne Cobbler	181
Santinas Pousse Cafe	181
Sherry Wine Punch	183
Saratoga Cocktail	193
Sherry and Egg	196
St. Croix Crusta	197
Soda Cocktail	198
St. Croix Rum Punch	200
Soda Lemonade	200
St. Croix Fix	203
Soldiers' Camping Punch	213
Saratoga Brace Up	213
Sherry Wine and Ice	214
Shandy Gaff	217
Sherry Wine and Bitters	225
Stone Wall	229
Stone Fence	229
Sherry Wine Sangaree	229
Soda and Nectar	231
Soda Negus	233
St. Croix Sour	241

PAGE.
Sherry Wine Egg Nogg............................. 219
Star Cocktail....................................... 262
Silver Cocktail..................................... 262
St. Joseph Cocktail................................. 262

T

Toledo Punch....................................... 168
Tip Top Punch...................................... 184
Tom Collins.. 185
The Old Delaware Fishing Punch..................... 185
The American Champagne Cup......................... 214
Tom and Jerry (cold)............................... 226
Trilby Cocktail.................................... 242
Tea Punch for the Winter........................... 246
Tea Cobbler.. 251
Turkish Sherbet.................................... 258
Thorn Cocktail..................................... 261
Tenderloin Reviver................................. 265
Tuxedo Cocktail.................................... 267
Turf Cocktail...................................... 268

V

Vanilla Punch...................................... 171
Vermouth Cocktail.................................. 181
Virgin Strawberry Ice Cream........................ 258

W

Whiskey Daisy...................................... 167
Whiskey Rickey..................................... 171
White Lion... 172
Whiskey Crusta..................................... 179
Whiskey Julep...................................... 183
Whiskey Cocktail................................... 188

	PAGE.
Whiskey Sour	191
Whiskey Cobbler	195
Whiskey and Cider	217
Whiskey Fizz	227
Whiskey Fix	228
Wine Lemonade	230
White Plush	239
Wedding Punch for a Party	247
Whiskey Smash	255
Widow's Kiss	268
Wines with a Formal Dinner	269

1. HOW TO ATTEND A BAR.

The General Appearance of the Bartender, and How He Should Conduct Himself at All Times When on Duty.

The author of this work has, after careful deliberation, compiled the following rules for the management of a saloon, and would suggest the advisability of following these instructions while attending a bar. He has endeavored to the best of his ability to state them in perfectly plain and straightforward language, as the work must be conducted in the same systematic and proper manner as any other business. When waiting on customers, at any time, it is of the highest importance for a bartender to be strictly polite and attentive in his behavior and, especially, in his manner of speech, giving prompt answers to all questions as far as lies in his power; he should be cheerful and have a bright countenance. It is absolutely necessary to be neat, clean, and tidy in dress, as that will be more to the interest of the bartender than any other matter. He should be pleasant and cheerful with every one, as that will not only be gratifying to customers, but also prove advantageous to the bartender serving them.

It is proper, when a person steps up to the bar, for a bartender to set before him a glass of ice-water, and, then, in a courteous manner, find out what he may desire. If mixed drinks should be called for, it is the bartender's duty to mix and prepare them above the counter, and allow the customers to see the operation; they should be prepared in such a neat, quick, and scientific way as to draw attention. It is also the bartender's duty to see that everything used with the drinks is perfectly clean, and that the glasses are bright and polished.

When the customer has finished and left the bar, the bartender should clean the counter well and thoroughly, so that it will have a good, renewed appearance, and, if time allows the bartender to do so, he should clean, in a perfect manner, at once, the glasses that have been used, so as to have them ready again when needed. Regarding the bench which is an important feature in managing a bar properly, it is the bartender's special duty to have it cleared up and in good shape, at all times, for it will always be to his advantage if done correctly. (See illustration, plate No. 2.)

Other particular points are, the style of serving and the saving of time. Whenever you have to mix drinks which require straining into a separate fancy glass, such as cocktails, sours, fizzes, etc., make it a rule to place the glass of ice-water in front of the customer, next to it the glass into which you intend to strain the drink, and then go to work and mix the drink required; try to place your glassware on the counter all in one row or straight line. As to the personal style of the bartender, it is proper that, when on duty or while mixing drinks, he should stand straight, carry his head erect, and place himself in a fine position. (See illustrations, plates Nos. 1 and 3.)

2. HOW A BARTENDER MAY OBTAIN A SITUATION.

When a bartender is looking for a position or an opening, it is of great importance for him to present a neat, clean appearance. It is also proper for him, as soon as he approaches the proprietor, to be careful in his speech and expressions, not say too much, but wait until the prospective employer asks him questions to which he should reply promptly. Have good recommendations with you, if possible, or, at least, be able to prove by references that you are reliable and capable. In entering an office or restaurant, it is proper to take off your hat, and, especially, while talking to the proprietor—a much-neglected act of courtesy. Many people believe that they lower themselves by lifting their hats, but this is a mistaken opinion, as it is only a matter of etiquette, and shows proper respect. When the proprietor is a gentleman, you will find he will do the same, even before you have; perhaps, to show that he has the proper knowledge of what etiquette demands.

A bartender inquiring for a position should be cleanshaven, with clothes well-brushed, and shoes blacked; and should not speak to the proprietor with a cigar in his mouth, and neither should he spit on the floor, be chewing a toothpick, use slang or profane language, or indulge in other bad habits. All his answers should be short and in a polite tone of language.

When the question of wages is introduced, you must know yourself what you are worth, and every good bartender should demand good wages. Of course, it's much better to demand the proper salary, at once, than to accept small wages at the beginning, and then attempt to have it increased later, as this method generally creates an ill-feeling between employer and employee, especially if the desired "raise" is refused. It is advisable for the bartender to ask the proprietor or manager, in a gentlemanly manner, what hours he is to work, whether by day or night, whether entitled to meals or not, what privileges are to be given him, what is demanded of him, and obtain information of all the particular rules and regulations governing the place of business. If everything is satisfactory to both, and you have been engaged, at once leave the place, in a proper manner, and do not linger about, trying to occupy the proprietor's time more than necessary, and not give the bartender, who is going to leave or to be discharged, an opportunity to know what the business talk has been, or stop and chat to any possible acquaintance, who may be present, about what you are going to do.

I try to impress on every bartender's mind that he should study his business as much as possible, in every way, so that he be entitled to the highest salary paid; for I do not believe in cheap bartenders. It is much better for the proprietor to pay high wages to those fully understanding their business than to hire "shoemakers" who have but little if any knowledge of the business. Cheap men, as a rule, are worthless.

3. THE MUTUAL RELATIONS OF EMPLOYER AND EMPLOYEE.

It is important that the proprietor of a hotel, restaurant or saloon should try his best to get good help, the best to be obtained in his line of business, for the reason that the more skilled assistance he has in his employ, the easier it is to conduct the business, and the more successful he will be. After having secured a good set of employees, it is the proprietor's duty to pay them well, every one according to his position; treat them all with politeness, and set a good example by his own manner for them. For example:—When the proprietor enters his place of business in the morning, or at any other time, he should salute his people properly by bidding them the time of day, saluting with a pleasant nod, and create a genial feeling among them all by approaching and speaking to some one or more of them, calling them by name, as he may address them casually or on business. By doing this, he will create good feeling between the help and himself, and even in his absence his employees will do their work correctly and promptly. But, otherwise, by not treating them kindly, it can not be expected that the help will take any particular interest in the business or do more than is absolutely necessary to retain their situations. This indifference will naturally be detrimental to the business of the place. It is plainly apparent that when the help are not treated right, the proprietor acting harshly or with an overbearing manner, never having a "good word" for any one, lacking the commonest politeness of even saying "good morning!" he will fail to make a success; for his employees, instead of caring for his interests, will be antagonistic to him, caring little whether his business runs down or not. The fact is, that employers and employees, should be in harmony with one another, in every direction, the proprietor looking upon his help as friends, regarding them with a family feeling, while they should have the proper respect for him as an authorized boss, but with no fear, and, certainly, with no idea of treating him familiarly.

It is a sensible idea for the proprietor, from time to time, when doing a very successful business, to give his employees a little inducement in the shape of a raise of wages, proportionate to their different positions. This will cause them to strive more earnestly to benefit the business, and thereby benefit themselves. It is well also to be prompt in letting the employees go at the hour designated, and not detain them unless they are to be paid extra. The employees, too, are to be just as precise in going to work at the exact minute specified. There should be a perfect system of working hours, the time of which is not to be disregarded by either party. If the proprietor is particularly successful and making plenty of money, it is advisable to give also an occasional extra holiday, in proper proportion, providing the help is worthy of it from long and earnest service, or, if possible, in the summer season, to let the employees have, at different times, a brief vacation, though this is naturally a difficult matter in our line of business.

When the proprietor sees the time is fit to reward any one of the employees, to tender an extra present to some particular one, he should, if financially able, privately put a five or ten-dollar bill in the man's hands without any comment, and without letting others see the action. There should not be any self-praise—such an action brings its own reward—and, in this case, it is not well to let the left hand know what the right hand is doing. By such means, you will keep your good, faithful people with you, and be sure they are working to the best of their ability. Where the proprietor is not in the position of being able to reward financially his employees, a pleasant look, cheery words, and friendly actions will go far with those who can appreciate, and take, to some extent, at least, the place of a money gift. If the proprietor is successful, he should not display a pride of his own rise, and imagine it's all the result of his own brilliant mind, claiming entire credit for his financial progress, but acknowledge his indebtedness to his help, for without their assistance he would not have made such rapid advance on the ladder of success. Give encouragement to your help, but do not let them understand that it is by their efforts alone your business has prospered; for, if you flatter them too much, you can easily spoil the best of men in your employ. Never be bombastic or domineering, at any rate. It is very vulgar to be purse-proud. It is wise, under certain circumstances, to supply your help with meals, and, when it is practicable, it should be seen that the employees have good, substantial food, well cooked and properly served, and not have refuse or "leavings" given them, caring little when and how they get it. It is not necessary to furnish them with delicacies and luxuries, but food that will keep one in strength and proper physical condition, to the lowest as well as to the highest assistant in your employ. It is wise for the proprietor or manager to state the regulations of the house when hiring the help, insisting that they should be clean, energetic, sober, drink only a certain amount at meal time or between meals, as standard rules are more beneficial in their results, and will retain people much longer in their situations than where there are no regulations, and every one is allowed to do more or less, as they please. After all the facts mentioned and noting suggestions offered, it will be found that they will give satisfaction to both, the one hiring and to those who hire out. The proprietor is to remember that here the golden rule, "Do unto others, as you wish them to do to you," is of paramount importance.

In a large concern, where much help is employed, make it a rule that what are known as "officers" (the bartenders, cashier, assistant cashier, manager, headwaiter, etc.), are to be allowed to order from the bill of fare (where there is a restaurant attached) when they eat, and specify in your rules a certain amount they are entitled to order in value, perhaps from 40 to 60 cents, in price. When this is not done, many employees will ruin their stomachs, and, consequently, their health by over-feeding, and also create a bad feeling among themselves as well as with the other help, by taking special delicacies; the result being that the proprietor is ultimately forced to make the rule he should have had at first, and thus makes it very unpleasant for all the employees.

It is absolutely necessary for the proprietor to protect his people from insults or wrongful accusations by the customers. It is often the case when a patron is a little intoxicated, he may think he has the privilege of calling the employees any sort of a name, but it is then the proprietor's duty to step in and call the man to order. If the waiter is accused of wrong-doing, it is the proprietor's place to ascertain which one of the two is in error, and if he finds out the employee is in the right, he must defend and support him, at any risk, careless of what the results may be to himself. It is also the proprietor's or manager's duty to see that the "officers" eat properly, conduct themselves quietly, especially if in the public dining-room, so the guests will not be annoyed by any exhibition of bad or vulgar table manners. The boss should look after these matters with the same care he would supervise the control of his own family.

It is not the intention of declaring absolutely that any and every proprietor should do as I have written, but, naturally, use his own judgment in connection with these suggestions.

4. RULES FOR BARTENDERS IN ENTERING ON AND GOING OFF DUTY.

When the stipulated time arrives for a bartender to quit, it is his duty to see that his bench is in perfect order, that all his bottles are filled, that his ice-box has sufficient ice in it, that all glassware is clean, and everything straightened out in such a manner that when his relief arrives the latter will have no difficulty, and can immediately commence to serve customers.

When the relief takes charge, it is his duty to convince himself that nothing has been neglected, such as stock filled, bar stock replaced, empty bottles removed, and the proper pressure given to the beers, whether water, air or carbonated pressure. Sufficient fruit should also be cut up ready for use, and everything properly arranged to enable him to perform his duty satisfactorily. Where there is no cheque system, the cash must be properly arranged, also. This is generally done by the proprietor or the one having the management, so that there will be no difficulty in regard to the condition of the cash drawer, which is a most important point in business.

5. FIRST DUTY IN OPENING A BAR-ROOM IN THE MORNING.

The greatest attraction of a bar-room is its general appearance. The first thing a bartender should do is to open the place, every morning, promptly, on the minute, at the hour it is understood the saloon begins business. First give the place a perfect ventilation, and immediately after prepare your ice-water ready to meet the first demand. Put the porter to work, have him properly clean up the bar-room and water-closet floors without unnecessary raising of dust. After the floor is cleaned, have all the cabinet work, counters, cigar case, ice boxes, ceiling, chandeliers and globes (when necessary) cleaned and dusted thoroughly, the glasses and mirrors polished, and the windows washed. But only a moist sponge should be used on the fine cabinet woods which are then to be dried gently with a towel. The use of a great amount of water will injure the panels of wood-work especially. The silverware and glassware should be in perfect condition, clean towels supplied to closets, and napkins, towels, "wipers," and hand-towels to the bar. Then, turn your attention to the bottles containing liquors, mixtures, etc.; see that they are filled and corked, and those required for ready use placed on ice. Go to work on your bench, place all the glassware on top of the counter, but use as little space as possible, to give yourself plenty of room to wait on customers who might come in at that time. Next, give the bench a thorough scrubbing or washing, and, afterward, wash your glassware well in clean water, and place those that belong there back on the bench. After having your bar and all bottles cleaned and polished, see that your wines and liquors are cool and pleasant and in a proper condition. Have the ice boxes on the bench filled with fine-broken ice and stored with the necessary goods. Cut up the fruits—oranges, pine-apples, berries, and lemon-peel for cocktails—that may be needed during the day. The bartender should have this part of his work done as quickly as possible and make his appearance behind the bar, neat and clean, as soon as his work permits him, not looking half-dressed, in his shirt-sleeves, and in a general untidy appearance that is likely to drive away customers.

The filling of the glasses with ice water is an important item. In placing the glasses before a customer they should be clean and perfectly filled, but the best way is to hand out a clean, empty tumbler and a pitcher of ice water, allowing the customer to help himself.

Don't let the porter forget the water-closet seats, urinals, and wash-stands, and to put plenty of toilet paper, soap, etc., where needed. It is of importance to obtain the services of a first-class porter, as his work requires intelligent managing. A cheap man is worthless.

For disinfecting I recommend the use of hot water, containing common (wash) soda and, after thorough cleansing to create a good, sweet odor, the use of a piece of natural or artificial ice, the size of the bowl or basin. If it is thrown in, there is great danger of the

PLATE No. 1.

HARRY JOHNSON'S STYLE OF MIXING DRINKS TO A PARTY OF SIX.
Copyrighted, 1888.

breakage of the bowl, and, consequently, only a man of sensible judgment should be employed to do this kind of work.

6. WHY BARTENDERS SHOULD HAVE THEIR OWN UNION FOR PROTECTION AND ASSOCIATION.

In many long years of experience, I have tried several times to start an organization for the mutual benefit and protection of bartenders. The first attempt was made about 1875, in New Orleans, in an effort to procure for them sufficient wages, to give them a good, decent living, proper hours of labor, and for their general elevation as members of society. The effort at that time resulted unfortunately for the reason, principally, that the old, skilled bartenders, who retained the same situation for years, had passed away—men who supported well themselves, their families, and their clubs—and, in their stead, was a younger element in this avocation who, not knowing their work thoroughly, were careless and indifferent, and unable, drifted about from one place to another. The consequence was that they never became members of the club, and would not have been of benefit, had they done so. Under such circumstances, it was impossible to organize a beneficial society.

At the present time it is entirely different, for the reason that our business is regulated by prescribed rules; and bartenders should now have an association of mutual support, as well as the people of any other avocation. Nearly every man in the hotel and restaurant business belongs to some club or protective society; the cooks have their unions; the pastry cooks also a home and an association; the waiters have an organization; and there does not exist any valid reason why the bartenders should not have a similar combination. I claim that the last-named are as much entitled to certain rights as is the skilled mechanic and laborer, and this for many reasons. As we all know, the bartenders, as a rule, have never, with but few exceptions, had regular working hours. Neither have they had a regular and fixed salary paid according to their skill and knowledge of the business. It is perfectly natural that a poor bartender, with little understanding of his vocation, could not have the same amount of wages as a superior one working in first-class houses. Still, if this man is of good character and reputation, and honest, he could very readily become a very useful member of the club, provided he is willing to do what is right, live up to the regulations of the society, paying promptly his dues and assessments, as much so as the more skilful bartender. There must necessarily be second-rate as well as first-class men, and there are plenty of houses which can not always afford to pay for the services of a superior man, and must, therefore, take one of less ability. The principal endeavor for bartenders belonging to a club or organization is to attempt the moral and mental elevation and education of themselves to such a degree that the entire public will recognize them as gentlemen and useful business men of the community. Therefore, I recommend every bartender to take all opportunities to advance himself in every direction—not only good habits, good dressing, good manners, and clean appearance, but, also, to devote some of his spare time, at least, to reading what will help him; to associate with the best people possible, visit places that will be of benefit to him, try to study their own personal welfare as well as that of their families (if they have any), and set an example to his fellow-brethren and the world in general, in the full belief that he is as good a man as any one else who behaved himself, and can maintain a club or association that will compare favorably with any other. By doing all this, and having the mutual support of one another, it will be easier for those bartenders, who are in need of a situation, or are suffering from an accident or illness, to get along without fear of the future. It does not require a great amount of capital to start a beneficial institution. A place of meeting, one or more rooms, at a moderate rent, and no salaried officer, except the secretary, with some little expenditure for light and heat, will comprise the list of ordinary expenses. There will always be many members who will gladly serve in the various offices, satisfied with the honor, and without thought of any compensation. Besides the regular members, there are many other people, such as restaurant, hotel and café proprietors, who will sympathize with a body of this class, and will willingly give it their aid, in advice, hints, and suggestions, gratis. Individually, I would only be too glad to offer to such an association my services with all the advice and information I am capable of giving, at any time, whatever.

In considering the way some people in our line of business have been abused by heartless employers, who, by dumb luck, or, more often, entirely from the efforts and ability of their bartenders, have achieved a fortune, I can not be too severe. One of this type of men takes a notion to go out for his own amusement, and fashionably attired, with a big diamond in his shirt front and a large roll of bills in his pockets, possibly a horse and carriage at his disposal, he starts out on a day of sport, with no consideration for the welfare or feelings of his bartender, caring little, whether his employee works 8, 10, 12, or 18 hours that day, or whether he gets his proper meals, so long as he has a "good time;" the bartender, in many such cases, working for a small salary, and constantly being imposed upon by the proprietor who is only actively engaged in wasting his own money.

Therefore, bartenders should do what is best to protect themselves, and join together in an association of mutual help and endeavor. The members should ask only for wages that are reasonable, and never try to annoy their employers by threats of a strike, but have every difficulty, that may occur between the boss and the help, settled in a sensible manner, so that the business may not suffer by it. As soon as the men begin to dictate to their employers regarding wages and length of hours, they will fail, because they are not in the right, and they will not have the sympathy of the public. Our hours are always necessarily longer than those of the ordinary mechanic, but one should not be kept working in a continuous stretch of many hours. There are cases, naturally, where a man is obliged to stay on his post a few minutes longer than the allotted time, but no proprietor has a right to make a bartender work as long as he pleases, just because he thinks his "dispenser of drinks" is a slave. I have stood behind the bar in twenty years' active service, in various cities, and have been in business myself for twenty more years, so I have had the experience, the knowledge, and the feeling of parties to both sides of the question of employer and employee. A man who is fortunate enough to be a proprietor should be pleased to help his bartenders to obtain an organization, in which they may be financially and socially improved. Furthermore, bartenders joining an association of this nature, will find it of great advantage, as they can help each other in case of sickness, disability or death. I have known hundreds of good bartenders who, meeting with misfortune, became entirely destitute of friends and means. A new association should not start off under the impression that it can immediately begin to help largely its members, who are in need, with any great amount of benefits; but it will soon find out, that, under good business management, it will be on a firm financial basis. It is necessary to know that we must creep before we can walk.

As far as I am concerned, I wish such an association the best success in all its undertakings, and, under all circumstances, it will have my good will, and may count upon my friendship, provided that its officers and members act as men and gentlemen. I know how a man feels when he has to stand behind the bar, because there are no well-regulated hours, no prescribed regular salary for certain duties, and, then, one is frequently obliged to stand the insults and abuse, at times, of a certain class of customers. Why shouldn't we bartenders have a union and protect ourselves, and why shouldn't we be respected as well as any other man, so much the more so as it requires ability and a level head to become a first-class bartender, while a shoemaker is absolutely unfit for our business?!

A man in our line, to be successful, must be quick, prompt, courteous, able, a good student of human nature, a good dresser, clean, and possessing several more virtues. Therefore, a bartender should be respected and as well paid, proportionately, as a man in any other line of business. It is proof that we could not use every Tom, Dick, and Harry, because leading bartenders frequently command very large salaries. In my own case, I had for a number of years $100 a week paid to me. This is evidence that a man must know and have sufficient ability and scientific knowledge to fill the position, though every one is not as fortunate as myself, and I have worked for as low an amount as $15 a week, too.

Now, boys, do what is right, and stick together! If you do, you will soon better your own situations and chance in life.

7. GETTING YOUR MONEY WHEN BUSY OR IN A RUSH.

To get your money is the most important and leading point of the business, and, certainly, needs as strict attention as anything else. The correct way of doing this is to calculate the amount while preparing and serving the drinks. As soon as this is done, it is to be understood, without exception, that the man behind the bar, attending the customers, should immediately turn out the cheque or proper amount labeled on paper (out of the cash register), and then deliberately place it half-folded on the mixing shelf, at his station wherever he may serve the party. The cheque should not be placed out on the counter or bar, because some one of the party drinking may accidentally knock it off the bar, or forgetfully place it in his pocket without paying, and, then, in case of disagreement or argument between the bartender and the party drinking, whether the drinks had been paid or not, there would not be any proof either way. But on the mixing shelf the cheque is in the possession of the bartender, and under the eyes of the cashier, until it is paid, and thus there can not possibly be any cause for a dispute.

A piece of paper left flat may not readily be seen, lying on a desk or shelf, but half-folded or creased, it has ends that make it more visible. In case of a large rush, at the lunch, dinner or supper hour, or when the place is next to, or in the vicinity of, a theatre, public hall, circus, etc., where there would necessarily be a rapid trade, at certain hours, especially in the evening, the cashier not only takes the money handed him by the bartenders, but also keeps watch, as far as possible, that the proper amount of money is paid over by the different parties of customers. At these times it is the duty of the proprietor or manager to place himself in such a position that he can oversee all that is being done, help to rectify mistakes, and notice, also, that probably the right amount of money is being handed in. This is not because the proprietor is doubtful of the honesty of his employees, but because it is his duty to exercise for his own benefit a careful supervision of his own business.

Whenever there is such a rush, it is proper for the bartender, as soon as he receives money from the customer, in payment for the drink, to pick up the cheque and immediately crie out the change desired; for instance, if the bill is 40 cents, and a dollar bill was presented, he would say, *"Forty out of a dollar!"*—as this saves time, if instead he waited until he got up to the cashier. By calling out, at once, the change is ready ordinarily for him as soon as he reaches the cashier. It is always the bartender's duty to be smart and quick, in order to get the money for the drinks, and allow no one to escape without paying. In making your own change, it is proper to hand the balance, due the customer, in a courteous manner to him, placing it on a dry spot of the counter, so that, if a mistake occurs, it can easily be rectified. The change should not be placed in a pile, but spread out in such a way that any error, of too much or too little, can quickly be seen by both, bartender and customer.

8. HINTS ABOUT TRAINING A BOY TO THE BUSINESS.

For the last thirty years of my experience, I had the opportunity of training many hundreds of boys to our trade, and would suggest to any proprietor, manager or bartender to treat the boy strictly, teaching him manners and restrain him from becoming impudent to you or to the customers. I would advise that the man behind the bar give the boy all particular points and information regarding the business, talk to him in a pleasant, but still authoritative way, and don't let him hear bad language, if it is possible to avoid it. See that he always looks neat and clean, and have him obey your orders fully. Meanwhile, give him the liberty that properly belongs to him and, by doing so, you will turn out a very good, smart, and useful boy, fit for your business. Whenever you have the opportunity, it is your duty to set a good example to him; teach him as much as you are able, so that when he is grown he can call himself a gentleman, and need not be ashamed of his calling.

A good many people, I am sorry to say, are laboring under the erroneous impression that there is no such thing as a gentleman in the liquor business. If those people, however, knew thoroughly the inside operations of our avocation, or became acquainted with some good man employed therein, they would soon come to the more proper conclusion that none but gentlemen could carry on the liquor business in a strict and systematic way. The trouble is that most of these narrow-minded people have no accurate information on the subject, and, consequently, are led to place all men in our business under the same heading.

9. TREATMENT OF PATRONS—BEHAVIOR TOWARD THEM.

The first rule to be observed by any man acting as bartender is to treat all customers with the utmost politeness and respect. It is also a very important matter to serve the customers with the very best of liquors, wines, beers, and cigars that can be obtained; in this respect, naturally, one must be governed by the style of house kept and the prices charged. Show to your patrons that you are a man of sense and humanity, and endeavor to do only what is right and just by refusing to sell anything either to intoxicated or disorderly persons, or to minors. If you think a customer is about spending money for a beverage, when it is possible that he or his family needs the cash for some other, more useful purpose, it would be best to give him advice rather than the drink, for which he has asked, and send him home with an extra quarter, instead of taking the dime for the drink from him. The customers will then respect you as a gentleman and a business man. No one should make distinctions between patrons on account of their appearance. As long as they behave like gentlemen, they should be treated as such. Therefore, all customers, whether rich or poor, should be served alike, not only in the same respectful manner, but with the same quality of goods; not keeping a special bottle for rich people, and an inferior grade for poorer persons, unless you have before you one who prefers quantity to quality. In observing these rules, you will build up a reputation as a first-class business man who acts with correct principles, and you will find it safe and easy to succeed. But there is a way of spoiling your customers, and that is by offering too much or by treating too often. This latter fault is especially the case with many on opening a new place of business. It is always the wisest to give your customers all they are entitled to, but no more.

10. HOW TO IMPROVE THE APPEARANCE OF BAR AND TOILET ROOMS.

It is the duty of a bartender to keep everything connected with the bar-room in such a manner that it will attract the attention and admiration of customers and visitors. A clean condition will also aid in preserving the pictures and ornaments. Have the fixtures oiled, occasionally, using good, raw linseed oil, but not too much of it. Woodwork should be thoroughly cleaned and dried, before the oil is used on it. I have often been in places where they lavish their entire attention on one particular thing to the detriment of all others, and especially the toilet-room, which is one of the most important matters to be kept in the best order. In fixing up a new place or altering an old one, it is advisable to have the toilet on the same floor as the café, if there is room for it, and proper facilities that it may receive constant observation and, consequently, proper attention. My advice to the proprietor of a public place is that he sees that the toilet-rooms are comfortably heated as well as ventilated, in the winter time, that there may not be danger of the water pipes freezing. This is not only annoying, but very expensive, in having the necessary repairs made. In summer, the toilet-rooms should be well lighted, with a supply of fresh air, at all times. These rules should always be strictly observed. Where ample space can be devoted to the toilet-rooms, a wash-stand, mirror, clean towel, brush, comb, and cuspidors, with plenty of toilet paper, will add to the comfort of the patrons of the establishment. And from time to time —perhaps, once a fortnight—the closets should receive a thorough overhauling and cleansing.

Where there is sufficient room, it is very advisable to have the closets as large as possible. They should contain two or more hooks for the convenience of cus-

PLATE No. 2.

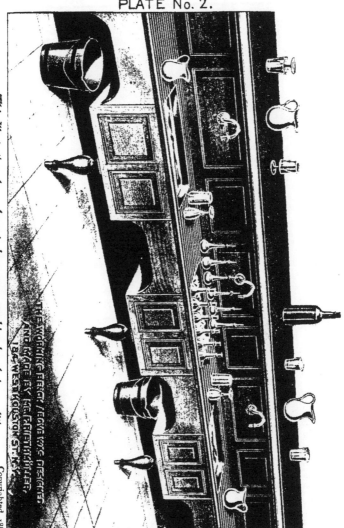

This Illustration shows how to keep your working bench in condition.

Copyrighted, 1888.

tomers, by which they can hang up their hats and coats. In a large establishment it is best for the proprietor to have a man stationed about the toilet-rooms to keep them in condition, and to wait upon those needing paper, soap, and other requirements.

11. TO KNOW HOW A CUSTOMER DESIRES HIS DRINK TO BE MIXED.

The greatest accomplishment of a bartender lies in his ability to exactly suit his customer. This is done by inquiring what kind of a drink the customer desires, and how he wishes it prepared. This is especially necessary with cocktails, juleps, "sours," and punches. The bartender must also inquire, whether the drink is to be made stiff, strong, or medium, and then must use his best judgment in preparing it; but, at all times, he must make a special point to study the tastes of his customers and, strictly heeding their wishes, mix all drinks according to their desires and taste. In following this rule, the barkeeper will soon gain the esteem and respect of his patrons.

12. HINTS FROM THE AUTHOR.

The author of this work would like to make a few remarks in relation to a special furnishing that has generally been greatly neglected. Whatever saloon or café you visit, you will find, with but few exceptions, no matter how elegantly the place is fitted up, that the working bench is usually constructed in a very poor and ill-shaped manner. Now, the remedy recommended is, that whenever a party has a saloon or bar-room fixed up for business, he should not leave all the arrangements to the cabinet-maker but make it a special point to have the bench constructed in a neat and comfortable method, and of sufficient width, so that it will "show off" and be handy at the same time, especially in regard to the liquor, ice and water boxes. Every working bench should be lined with copper and tinned over, and made of the best materials. This fixture cannot be made too well and it is best to not spare expense in having it done. With the copper lining the bench will last much longer, practically forever, and there is avoided not only the unpleasant leaking but the continual repairs that a cheaper bench will constantly require. The various boxes should be made with rounded edges, as square ones accumulate dirt and are, necessarily, more difficult to clean. Every box should have a false or loose bottom—a sheet of copper is preferable—the same size as the box, as this prevents injury to the real bottom of the box. The top lining of the bench should be corrugated, with a slight pitch forward, that the water may run off rapidly. The size of the liquor box depends upon the size of the bench. If a large business is expected, ample provision should be made for it. When expecting to do a fair business, the liquor box should be large enough to hold the principal liquor bottles that are supposed to be kept cool. For instance, at each end of the box there should be sufficient room for two or three bottles of whiskey—the 15-cent as well as the 10-cent grade—two bottles of gin (Old Tom and Holland), two bottles of sherry and Rhein wine, a couple of bottles of siphon seltzer as well as a bottle or two of imported seltzer. The box should be made of sufficient depth that the bottles will fit in the tubes, so that only the necks will appear to sight. The proprietor must know when he gives the order to the cabinet-maker, whether he wants the box to contain eight, ten or twelve bottles. The ice-box containing the broken or shaved ice should also have an extra bottom made of wood, in order that neither the true bottom nor the ice-pick should be injured by contact with one another. The wood bottom should be perforated, so that the drainage and lees may run off readily. All the bottles in use should always be kept closed with good corks, and covered with nickel or sliver-plated mountings. The face of the bench should be decorated with good cabinet-work, in order to cover the rough material which is generally used, and, furthermore, the legs or supports should be "turned," instead of the wide boards generally seen, for the reason that more room is obtained, cleaning is easier and the effect is naturally more pleasing to both the eyes of proprietor and customer. The floor underneath the working bench should be kept scrupulously clean, nothing being placed there except a fancy waste pail for each station. A handsome box of the same material as the cabinet work, lined with copper or other proper metal, is to be placed on the floor underneath the bench, for the purpose of placing empty bottles in it. The box-lining will save much labor and prevent accumulations of "leavings." Additionally, every bar systematically arranged should have a couple of boxes made of the same material as the cabinet work, to be placed on the floor under the bench as a receptacle for the corks. Every bench should have the tubes in the liquor box, and exact measurements should be taken, allowing for the width of the bottles as well as the space occupied by each tube. For instance, if the liquor box is to contain ten bottles of four inches diameter each, the box must necessarily be more than forty inches in length. Formerly, the tubes were made of wood which, continually damp, would, in the course of time, give out a bad odor. I have, therefore, invented these metal tubes, which should also be perforated, as this condition will more naturally admit the cool air to the bottle, keep it from sweating and have the liquor in a proper temperature for instant use.

No bartender should expectorate or throw bits of paper or other refuse into any of these tubes. By refraining from so doing, absolute cleanliness is assured. Expense should not be spared in making a handsome and convenient working bench, as far as one's finances will allow, for it is the chief feature of the place, and it should be the proprietor's pride to have this part of his establishment a source of gratification to both him and the public. Again, in a bar-room where the working bench has not sufficient natural light, artificial means should be used. The small expense of lighting up a dark bench will be saved in the prevention of breaking bottles and glassware. It is also to be remembered that the bench should be large enough to allow the placing of bottles between the bench and the top of the counter. The apertures—from eight to twelve in number—for the bottles, which are usually from $3\frac{1}{2}$ to 4 inches wide, should be made so that the end ones will come exactly to the edge of the board and not leave room for the possible accumulation of refuse. Have the sugar box or bowl arranged so that it can be conveniently reached, thus losing neither time nor steps. The floor behind the bar should be clean and kept perfectly dry. This will likewise be beneficial to the health of the man doing work behind the bar. The edge of the bench should be covered with a strip of metal $1\frac{1}{2}$ inches wide, and this, when polished, will "show off" the bench to advantage.

13. THE OPENING OF A NEW PLACE.

The most important thing to be looked after in opening a new place is its location. The more prominent the position, the more benefit you will derive from it, and the easier it will be for you to obtain trade. The next step is for you to obtain as long a lease as possible, provided you have faith in your projected enterprise. Don't start in on a short lease. The chances are too great against you. Just at the period your business has become successful, your lease for a short term may have expired, and the landlord may refuse to renew the lease or raise your rent to such an exorbitant figure that there would be little opportunity left you for profit.

Be sure and have the ordinary clause that would prevent you from sub-letting or selling your business omitted from the lease contract. The opportunity might be offered you to sell your business at a fancy price, and you want to be in position to do as you please, if possible, without asking your landlord's consent. Still, always try to be on good terms with him. It should also be definitely stated in the lease who pays the taxes, water tax and insurance, and who is responsible for repairs. You may otherwise find many extras added to the rent you have supposed covered the entire expense to you.

Furthermore, the tenant should ascertain whether the building has been condemned or whether the Board of Health has any cause of action against the premises, or whether there is anything in the neighborhood detrimental to the success of a respectable business. Above all, be certain before you sign a lease whether the Board of Excise or the proper authorities will license the place.

The next step is to fit up the rooms or building in a style suitable to the neighborhood. If it is a superior one, your furnishings must necessarily be elegant and costly. If in a poorer locality, the fixtures should be accordingly. But opening in a new locality, wherever it may be, it is wise to avoid spending too much in the arrangement and embellishment of the place, as there may not be the patronage expected nor the opportunity to sell the place at any profit.

Then select good mechanics—carpenters and cabinet-makers—because you need good work and must expect to pay a fair figure for excellent workmanship. Cheap woodwork will easily be injured and quickly destroyed. After securing the services of the cabinet-maker, you should select the style of counter top, which should be of the best lumber, thoroughly seasoned, worked out, filled, and oiled sufficiently long before to be in proper condition when you are ready for opening. If you neglect to have the counter top done till the last moment, it will be impossible to have it in proper shape, and by use it will soon be reduced to a horrible condition.

Sometimes, unfortunately, the proprietor is not able to furnish the place sufficiently well for the location. This is liable to cause him a loss of trade. Again, in a cheap neighborhood, where there is no possible chance of return for the investment, he may expend too much money in fixing up his place of business. The proper method of doing must naturally be left to every man's good judgment. Next find the proper place for your cellar and wine room. The cellar is, literally, the foundation of success. It should be properly ventilated, and, if possible, have a good cemented floor. At the earliest moment, lay in your ales and porter, as they require weeks to get settled. If you delay putting them in the stock until the opening day, they are likely to be a muddy-looking beverage when opened for use.

While making arrangements to open your business it is best to try to gain the good will of the people about you and of as many prospective customers as possible.

There are other legal requirements also to be noticed by the intending proprietor. In New York State, no saloon is allowed within 200 feet of a church or school, and other States have special laws defining the location of a saloon, restaurant or hotel.

The question of expense and profits may be indicated as follows (and, before entering business, it is well to take into consideration that there are usually only six working days in the week or three hundred and thirteen in the ordinary year):

For a good location, in our larger cities, the rent would be about $5,000 per annum or, daily, about	$16.00
Daily wages for six men required—	
Two bartenders, at $15.00 weekly	
One lunchman, at $15.00 "	
One cashier, at $12.00 "	
One porter, at $10.00 "	
One boy, at $10.00 "	12.83
Meals to employees (six, at 40c. each)	2.40
Drinks for the help, at meals	1.00
The "free lunch"	5.00
License (ordinarily $800 per annum)	2.28
Revenue tax	.08
Gas (or light)	1.50
Ice	1.50
Laundry	.50
Breakage	1.00
Coal	.50
Insurance	.25
Water tax	.25
General taxes	.50
Extras	1.00
The stock used would be about	40.00
Total	$86.59

These figures are only approximate, naturally, and as it may be rightly supposed such a business would have cash receipts of $100 every day, the profit would be about $13.40 daily. In a year, the profits would be 313 times $13.40 or $4,194.20. The chief point is always to be liberal in the allowance for expenses, and there is then the possibility of greater profits than were expected. Of course, it is not absolutely essential that the proprietor should furnish meals to his employees, but it is generally good business tact to keep them in the place continually and not miss possible trade when there is "a rush" or when their absence would possibly entail a loss of custom.

Whenever a man has a chance to run his place on Sundays, when it is not in violation of the law, it is advisable to do so, and, by the reducing of expenses creates an additional profit. It is to be understood that all the figures given only indicate the usual expenses of an establishment for which a rent of $5,000 per annum is paid. Where a larger rent is paid, both expenses and receipts are in larger proportion, though not necessarily, and where the moderate rent of $1,000 or $500 yearly is paid, they are in lesser degree. It frequently happens, however, in the business district of large cities that a small, admirably located place will do a great trade within what are known as "business hours."

14. HAVING A COMPLETE PRICE LIST.

It is the proper thing for every public house to have a plain and distinct price list—a wholesale list for the proprietor or manager, and a retail one for the cashier and the bartenders behind the bar. Also a special price list of different drinks, plain and mixed, in which every item, such as bottled goods, wines, clarets, champagnes, cordials, fancy beverages, in more or less quantities, quarts, half quarts, etc., should be distinctly specified. These lists will be found very advantageous, and will help to avoid many mistakes, especially in the sale of bottled goods, or when the barkeeper is a stranger behind the bar and not thoroughly informed in regard to the general prices. Without them the bartender finds it impossible to act justly toward both his employer and the customer or party to whom he sells.

15. TO KEEP ANTS AND OTHER INSECTS OUT OF MIXING BOTTLES.

Some bartenders find it difficult to keep insects out of the mixing bottles, although it is an easy matter if they take a small china or glass dish, pour some water into it, and place the bottle containing the syrup, cordial, etc., in the centre of it, which thus prevents the insects from getting to the bottle. When the bottles are left standing over night, or even during the day-time, for some hours, without using, put a little wooden plug into the mouth of the squirt or take the squirt stopper out and replace it by an ordinary cork until you use the bottles again.

Of course, it is understood that placing the bottle in a little dish of water is only necessary at night, on Sundays and on holidays, or, whenever the place is closed to business. In the day-time, as the bottles are in constant use, they do not require such attention, and keeping them in water would not only be a nuisance, by the dripping upon floor and counter, but also create too much moisture. It is wise not to purchase too much of the mixtures as gum, etc., because they can always be obtained on very short notice, and a large quantity on hand is likely to be injured by insects and from other causes long before use.

16. HANDLING OF CHAMPAGNES AND OTHER WINES.

Champagne baskets or cases should be opened carefully and the bottles placed on the shelves in a horizontal position to avoid breakage. Not more than is needed for immediate use should be placed on ice, but if more has been put on ice than should be called for it should not be removed, as it will lose strength and flavor, if allowed to get warm and then be returned to the ice. If left there, it should be kept at a temperature close to the freezing point, and the bottles placed so that the labels are not spoiled by ice or water. The bartender must handle champagne carefully, for on account of the gas contained in this wine the bottles break easily. Champagne as well as other wines—Rhine, Moselle, Sherry, Port, Claret, etc.—should be laid down when storing away. Every brand should be stored separately in the department to which it belongs.

17. CLEANING SILVERWARE, MIRRORS, ETC.

It will be found a simple matter to clean silverware by observing the following suggestions: Take a metal dish of lukewarm water, add a little soap, then put in your silverware, clean off all the foreign substance and then dry with a towel. Next, take No. 2 whitening, dissolve it thoroughly in water or spirits, apply

HARRY JOHNSON'S STYLE OF STRAINING MIXED DRINKS TO A PARTY OF SIX.
Copyrighted, 1888.

it in a thin layer, let it get dry, then rub it off with a towel and polish off with a chamois skin. If unable to reach the crevices with the chamois use a silver brush until every particle of whitening is removed. In cleaning mirrors, rub very quickly the glass with a damp towel until every spot is removed, and then polish with dry towel until the mirror is clean and bright. Use nothing but linen towels, the same as are always used with glassware. Particular attention must be given to the damp towel, and not have it wringing wet, for the simple reason that if it is too moist the water will get into the cracks and joints of the mirror frame. The excessive dampness, no matter how apparently trifling, will cause defects to the back surface of the mirror and eventually destroy it. In cleaning windows, in front of the store or restaurant, the porter, bartender, waiter or whoever may be employed to do it, should first dust off all the woodwork before beginning to clean the glass. There is nothing better than a clean towel dipped in plain water to wash off the surface of windows, fan-lights, etc. All this cleansing work should be done the first thing in the morning, before the time for customers to appear. Particular notice must be taken not to clean glass when the sun is shining upon it, as the reflections will spoil the best as well as the poorest of plate or common glass. It should be the pride of a man keeping a public place that the entire front of his establishment, containing plate or bevel glass, should look perfectly clean and brilliant, for people are thus able to judge from the exterior of the proprietor's character and disposition. They will also be able to form an opinion of the character of the place by the condition of the closets when visiting the rooms.

Furthermore, in cleaning your front windows, the chandeliers (hanging or stationary), the brass and metal work, the shades and globes, and where there are swinging or removable fixtures, they must be handled carefully or they will soon become easily injured, gas will escape, and to the annoyance will be added extra expense. If there is any brasswork connected with the front kick-plates as well as the push-plates, metal handles, hand or foot rails, lamp posts, hinges, frames and lamps, it should all be cleaned and polished before business begins in the morning. Done at a late hour, the work is an obstruction and nuisance to customers, and badly impresses the passer-by.

18. HOW CORKS SHOULD BE DRAWN FROM WINE BOTTLES.

The proper way to draw a cork from a wine bottle is first to cut off the top of the tin-foil cap, as far down as the rim, just below the groove in the neck of the bottle. This prevents any sediment or dust that may have been beneath the tin-foil from entering the wine as it flows out. The remainder of the cap remaining on the bottle presents also a good appearance. Then draw the cork. How bottled wine should be served has already been previously stated.

No bartender or waiter should ever think of pouring out wine with the left hand—in Europe, generally, this action is considered a personal insult or affront—because it is naturally awkward, except with a left-handed man, and even when the bottle is properly retained in the right hand, there is a correct way of grasping it, in order to have full control of the flow of wine and prevent spilling or any form of accident. Proper care should be taken of all empty bottles, and, if not returned, they should be sold to get a return of some part of their cost.

19. GLASSWARE FOR STRAINED DRINKS.

Attention must be given to have your glasses of the right size and style, sufficiently large to hold the mixed drinks—but not too large—you intend to strain into them. Mixed drinks will show to better advantage if served in a handsome style of glassware.

In every first-class, well regulated place it should be the pride of the man in charge to have nothing but the best selected glassware, a proper glass for every different kind of wine as well as for the mixed drinks. It is important in purchasing your glassware to consider the style of your house and the nature of your customers, because there are different grades of patrons everywhere. It is naturally understood that the finest glassware adds to the pleasant appearance of the surroundings of a café, restaurant or saloon, but a proper distinction must always be made. A man who has not a first-class trade should never purchase Bohemian or French glassware, which is exceedingly costly. The domestic manufacture which resembles the foreign goods can be obtained much cheaper.

20. THE ICE-BOX IN YOUR BASEMENT OR CELLAR.

It is very important for a man in our business to select the proper place for the ice box. He must be very careful and not have it placed where there is just beneath, or in the immediate vicinity, a number of pipes, such as steam, waste, water or sewer, for in case of their getting out of order, with the consequent necessary repairs, he would be given a vast amount of annoyance and trouble. The place where the box is to be placed should be perfectly dry and well ventilated. The box should be made of the best material, long and large enough, and sufficiently convenient to serve the purposes of your present trade, and even larger than the present demands, to meet the possible requirements of a growing business. It is much better to have it built sufficiently large for the future time so that you may not be troubled by having it enlarged or altered.

The ice box should not be nailed together, but built in sections, which are joined together by screws. It might happen that it was necessary to remove the ice box to some other place, and this could readily be done when it is in sections. Otherwise you would destroy the box in tearing it apart. The bottom of the box should, particularly, be made of the best lumber. Before the bottom of the box is filled with charcoal or sawdust, it is proper to put in a layer of good, solid felt paper, on both sides of the wood, so that the filling is packed between the two layers of paper. This will prevent air or heat from entering in between the cracks and crevices which would obviously heighten the temperature and evaporate the cold air. The side walls of the box should be made the same as the bottom, and they should reach as high as the ceiling of the basement or cellar, unless the ceiling is extraordinarily high. In that case, the box should be made the average height, which is about six feet six inches. The vacant space above the box should be boarded, filled, and boxed up with felt paper, right against the ceiling, in order to keep the hot air from settling down on the top of the box.

When you are obliged to have a large-sized box for your business, it may be possible that one door is not enough, when, of course, two should be made. Have the ice chamber constructed so that it will only come down as far as to allow the placing of barrels underneath it. If it is made too low down, the space underneath is wasted, as no keg or barrel can be placed there, and in an ice box you want every inch of room to be utilized. This chamber should also be made of the best material, the beams placed in it not crossed vertically but horizontally. The best material is hard pitch pine, the reason being that it does not absorb water, will neither rot nor decay, nor become filled with the bad odor as is frequent with soft woods. The drip-pan, to be placed under the ice chamber, must be of the proper size, not too small, or else water will drip outside of it. It should be made of galvanized iron or copper, for if cheaper material is used it will soon corrode and even break from the coldness of the water. As this furnishing of a place is only made once in a series of years, no expense should be spared in having the ice box constructed thoroughly and properly. The connections, such as the waste pipe, connected with the sewer should be made in such a manner that when it becomes closed up by the slime, as it will do in summer every ten days or fortnight, it can be easily taken apart, cleaned and then put together with but little trouble.

A small platform made of strong material, about two or three inches from the floor of the box, should run lengthwise in the rear and at the two ends, but should not obstruct the passage through the door or doors. The platform should be boarded up tight in front or else left perfectly open underneath, so that it will be easy to clean the vacant space. The top of the platform should be covered with smooth, solid galvanized iron to protect it, and also to allow a barrel to be slipped or pushed along on it with convenience.

Every first-class ice box should have one or two ventilators, placed conveniently, so that they can be regulated handily, in necessary changing of temperature as desired. On the floor inside of the box, close to the door or doors, a solid piece of iron or steel plate should be screwed, the same width as the door. This will not only prevent the heavy beer barrels from injuring the floor but keep it in good condition. Iron or steel plates, like a cornice, should be placed in all the four corners of the box to prevent the entrance of air. Not more than a quarter of an inch in thickness, they should always be screwed into the wood. A plate should also be attached to the inside of the doors, as well as to the door of the ice chamber, by screws, so that it will, when the door is closed, cover the crevice between the door and the jamb. Then there should be the proper size door plates made to cover the sills, and substantial door hinges, handles and knobs. When this is entirely completed, well put together and screwed up tight, have the box painted with two or three coats to suit your own taste, though I prefer white, as it helps to lighten the basement or cellar.

On the inside of the box, if there is room, have shelves put up at the top, on which to place bottled goods. At each end there should be a small shelf for your tools, such as mallet, brace and bit, a can containing plaster of paris and a bottle of water for mixing the plaster, the latter to be used if any of the beer barrels are leaking. If it is convenient, illuminate the ice box with electricity; if not, a candlestick and candle is to be placed on the shelves with matches ready for use. It is also best to have a small iron chain attached to the door, and a hook or staple, to which it can be fastened, when beer is being placed inside, so that the door will not constantly swing to, half closed. It is also wise to put to the bottom of the box, on the outside, good solid metal plates about five or six inches high (the height of the base), for the reason that it helps to preserve the box and keeps out the rats and mice who might otherwise gnaw into the box. It is to be understood, naturally, that the box should be kept clean and the bottom perfectly dry, as this will result in maintaining a sweet odor, with your stock in proper condition.

It is not to be forgotten that a good, reliable thermometer is always to be placed in the ice box, that the right temperature may be secured.

21. HOW TO HANDLE PROPERLY LIQUORS IN CASKS OR BOTTLES.

In laying in your imported liquors, I would not advise the purchasing of too great a quantity because, of late years, the consumption of imported liquors has decreased considerably, and by having too many packages on hand, ten per cent. or more of which will evaporate during the year, the original cost will be greatly increased. In a business where there is little demand for imported liquors, the wisest method is to buy in very small quantities or "case goods." As every one knows, in our line of business, imported liquors with the present high tariff are very costly, and the sensible man will only have a small stock on hand, being sure to purchase his goods from a reliable house —as otherwise he may get adulterated stock—and thus be certain that his customers are getting the best the market affords.

But where there is sufficient business to justify the laying in of foreign liquors in bulk, they should be placed together on the skid in one particular section of the cellar or wherever you may choose to keep them.

Before they are placed on the skid, the barrels should be stood up on end and a hole bored large enough for a faucet. Then have the barrels placed on the skid in such a manner that they cannot be shaken or jarred,

It is also wise to put a little tag inscribed with the name of the goods on each separate barrel, that you may readily know which liquors you desire may be found. It is furthermore advisable, in drawing liquor from the barrel or cask, not to loosen the bung, but to bore a small hole on top with a gimlet to give sufficient vent for the liquor to run freely out of the faucet. After having finished filling the bottles, place a little plug in the small hole made by the gimlet.

In handling domestic goods, such as American whiskies, etc., place them on a separate skid in the storeroom or cellar, after the faucet has been put in position. Give the liquor plenty of time to rest and settle before you start to draw vent. The same rule applies to the imported goods.

The temperature of the store-room (for both domestic and imported liquors) should never be less than from 60 to 65 degrees.

In handling "case goods" or bottled liquors (which are now in the fashion, I am sorry to say), you can either have your bottles standing up or lying down on your shelves, as it does not matter materially. I prefer the standing-up method, because it makes a better show, and you can more easily see whether there is anything missing or lacking. Try to have all your different brands—no matter what number—in separate places so that it will be convenient for you to find them instantly, at a moment's notice.

22. A FEW REMARKS ABOUT CASE GOODS.

Of late years it has become quite the fashion to sell over the different bars all the various brands of liquors or case goods. No one is to blame for this more than the proprietors or saloon-keepers, because every one of them, in the desire to offer special inducements and to obtain trade, have pushed these goods on to the public notice, and by so doing have cut into their own flesh. By offering and introducing the different brands, whether they were called for or not, and without stopping to think whether it was advisable or profitable to do so or not, people in our business have injured themselves and the trade as well.

A very large number of distilleries have introduced case goods at the expense of the proprietors of saloons and restaurants. When a man buys whiskeys, for instance, at from $2.50 to $3.00 a gallon for 10-cent goods, he has the chance to make a very handsome profit. But the majority of wholesale dealers now put up the same article in case goods and charge an enormous price for it. The average price of case goods is from $10 to $14 a case. With the dozen bottles in the case, at a cost of $12, the price would be $5 per gallon. That is, we must pay for the labels, the fancy bottles, and the immense amount of advertising in newspapers, by circulars, etc. Although people selling at retail, can very seldom get more than 25 cents for two, an average of $12\frac{1}{2}$ cents a drink, they are also obliged to cater to those customers who never take a whiskey without a glass of ginger ale, soda, seltzer, or other mineral waters, which reduces your profit materially, as the side-drink is always a gift. You can always figure that whenever you sell a case containing twelve bottles of whiskey, that there is always a case or more of some kind of a mineral water given away with the liquor. Consequently, it puts the price of your whiskey at an advance of from 70 to 75 cents a gallon.

Another bad feature of the use of case goods is, that with people who drink, they are no longer satisfied with an average amount, but take a large-sized drink, in order to have it "stiff" enough when mixed with the mineral water. It is also a mistake in showing and placing the case goods on the back-bar, where every one can see them, for it offers an inducement to every one to drink them, and is naturally, at any time, a temptation for the customer to call for them. I should advise any one, who is compelled to handle case goods, not to expose them to public view, but keep them in a closet where they are hidden from sight, but, if called for, of course, they must be produced.

The way our business is conducted, at present, it is understood that places can not be run without having more or less case goods; therefore, I recommend every first-class establishment to keep the leading brands of whiskey to suit all the varied tastes of your customers, if it is necessary to do so. I am sorry to state, that many people are not acting honorably with the public, and do not always give the goods that are asked for by the customers. Some get a few brands of different case goods simply for the purpose of obtaining the original bottles, and, when these bottles are first emptied, later fill them with any ordinary liquor, dealing it out under the label of the original goods. This is a very cheap form of swindle, and can not be too thoroughly denounced. Even if you are not able to make a fair profit, at least give the customer what he supposes is going to be handed out to him.

Where case goods are kept in a closet, the bottles in a front row, each brand should be four or five bottles deep, so that when the first bottle is emptied, the second of that special brand can be pulled forth by the bartender, the cap cut, and the cork drawn, in the sight of the customer, proving to him that he is getting the genuine goods, and that you, at least, are not engaged in defrauding the public.

It is also wise for every proprietor to teach his bartenders, that they should not recommend case goods,

PLATE No. 4.

CHAMPAGNE COCKTAIL.

Copyrighted, 1888.

but the staple article you have in bulk goods, with the understanding that you sell as good a whiskey as possible. All this depends upon the style of your establishment. The wholesale price of the best bulk goods is from $3.25 to $4.00 and $5.00 a gallon. Even by paying the extreme high price of $4, you can readily see how beneficial it is to recommend your bulk goods, as they will then cost you about $2 less a gallon than the case goods. In a medium-sized business, where they only sell ten gallons a day, it amounts to $20 difference, or about $7,000 per annum. The entire remedy lies in the power of the proprietor, and it is with him whether to push and sell case goods, or to place before the public the merits of bulk goods. The former are not all superior to the latter. While the last-named improves daily within the confines of the barrel, there is no improvement of the case goods within the limits of the bottle. It is the fancy label and the winning exterior appearance of the bottle that has made the public think, they are getting a superior article, but, in nine cases out of ten, it is not so. Therefore, I advise any man not to push the case goods more than possible, for he is only injuring his own business by doing so. I do not wish it to be understood that a proprietor should decline, at any time, to recommend case goods, but he should not disparage them, simply from a feeling of economy. All this particularly refers to imported goods, such as Scotch and Irish whiskey, in which the profits are so small and reduced, that if any one should sell only that class of goods, he would exist in business but a week. Some of the distilleries put up their older whiskeys in case goods, but, generally, they sell the same article both in case and in bulk goods.

23. A TIP TO THE BEGINNER.--HOW TO MAKE MONEY.

Any one going into our line of business starts, naturally, with the hope and intention of realizing profit; but it is not as easy as is generally supposed to make money and become very successful, although, more or less, every one imagines that he possesses all the qualifications required to conduct a thriving business. I have found it so, especially, with first-class bartenders, head-waiters, stewards, and head-cooks; the reason being that they think they have full knowledge of the business, in all its details. The fact that they are perfect in their specialty is not a proof nor a guarantee that they will be successful in managing a general business. On the contrary, it is the men who are so self-confident that usually fail. I have had in my employ thousands of people, bartenders, waiters, etc., and among these have been many brilliant men in their particular specialty or calling. But it is a sad truth that only a small percentage of these men, who have afterward begun business for themselves, have succeeded. There are various reasons for their failure. In some cases, these capable men were generally over-conceited, and that characteristic is not sufficient to give a control over all the different lines of our business. It does not necessarily prove, at least, that one has the qualifications to be a "boss." Others, such as very clever bartenders, who worked for a number of years in a first-class place and becoming very popular, came to the conclusion that the large extra trade there was entirely on their own account. They were led astray by taking a notion that they ought to open a similar establishment in the vicinity, because they were laboring under the conceited impression that all their friends and acquaintances would follow them, and give them exclusive patronage. I don't make these statements because of jealousy or narrow-mindedness, nor do I believe that no one should try to better himself. On the contrary, if a man thinks he can improve his financial condition by going into business for himself, he should do so, but he should not firmly believe that every one will flock to his new place, and give him the larger part of the trade, formerly held by his old "boss." All those people that make the bartender or head-waiter think they are such "good friends" usually fail in the hour of need, as they want special favors, attention, trust possibly, an occasional loan of money, and, in return, try to impress the bartender, head-waiter, etc., with the idea that they could do better for themselves in another position, that is, as proprietor. I admit there are lots of gentlemen who, taking a fancy to a bartender, or head-waiter, or steward, are sincere and honest in their advice when they counsel the men to do this; but all these points must be well-considered by every one who has the intention of going into business. One should, furthermore, consider if he is capable of competing with the neighboring cafés and restaurants, and whether he has sufficient means, plenty of stock of first-class quality; because his former proprietor has all these facilities, and, therefore, has always been able to please his customers, while the man in a new place must have time to demonstrate that he is also able to do it, always with some doubt whether he may be able to do so. Further advice to any one, especially in New York City, is this:—The bar-rooms, saloons, etc., up-town have longer hours than those down-town. For a beginner, to be sure of success, the chances are much better where longer hours prevail, for the reason that in the down-town places there is only a few hours' trade, and while your establishment there must be large, your expenses also, in comparison, will be large. If it should happen that you do not, in this place, have the "rush" at noon-time (from 11:30

A. M to 2 P. M.) you expected, there will not be any opportunity for making up the profit at any other time during the day; for, as a rule, there is no morning or evening trade. Additionally, you lose all the holidays and Sundays, for business-men are not down-town on such days, and, therefore, you can only count upon about 303 working days, out of 365 days in the year. The great drawback is, that you have to pay rent for the entire 365 days, pay wages to your help for the entire time, and that your running expenses are nearly as great as if you kept open every day in the year.

There are some few exceptions to this rule, of course, but such places are going out of the market, for the reason that the larger places will control the trade.

On the other hand, if a place is started where there are long hours, from 5 A. M. till an hour past midnight (New York law), the chances are much more in the beginner's favor; for, supposing he should have a slack trade in the morning or about noon, he may still have a good afternoon or night trade, or both, while his expenses are much less, proportionately, than the down-town places. This is what every one must consider well, before he starts in business. For instance: —Supposing a man finds a small place, where the expenses are $25 a day, and he is assured that he can take in $50 behind the bar. He may think this is a good business, but a little investigation will prove, that it is not. The price to him of the liquor consumed will be about $20. This, added to his running expenses, makes a total of $45, and leaves him just a net profit of $5 for the day; that is, $130 a month, and $1,560 a year. But he must pay for his living, and if a family is growing up around him, the $1,560 will only pay ordinary expenses, and give him a fair living. At the end of five or ten years, he will simply have lived well, probably not have saved any amount of money, and, as he has grown older, will possibly be less able to work hard. But if he pushes up the business to getting daily receipts of $75, he will then be progressing. His expenses will still be only $25, but, as the liquor he sells costs only $30, his daily expenditures are $55, which leaves him a profit of $20 a day. This is $520 a month, and $6,240 a year. If he works every day in the year, it is $7,300. Now, he can begin to save money, and, if shrewd and fortunate, may become a rich man. The point is, that it is useless to enter this business, unless one can make considerable money out of it.

So, if after coming to a conclusion that everything is more or less in his favor, and one makes the attempt, the responsibility for failure or success rests upon him alone. The leading and important points are for the man to have:—1st, good principles; 2d, a good system; 3d, to be capable of hard work and do it; and 4th, to be obliging and polite to every one. A beginner should not have in his place any card playing, or dice throwing, or any other special inducement, to draw trade, and get people to spend their money more than they would, if simply satisfying their thirst, for an ordinary, healthful amount of drink. Such inducements have both a bad effect and result upon business, especially on a new venture, because it doesn't look like a straight, legitimate way of getting the support of the public. During my many years of experience, I never allowed a pack of cards or a dice-box in my places. I do not intend to say that people should do as I have done, for this is only a declaration of my opinion. There are some places, where it is necessary to allow card-playing, because there are resorts where people are in the habit of playing cards in a family manner. It is perfectly necessary, that every one in our line of business should be courteous and pleasant, not only to his customers and his help, but to all other people, even to the newsboy, boot-black, or begging woman. Try to have a good word for all. If any one becomes a nuisance, get rid of them in a quiet manner. Don't refuse even an intoxicated man a drink (as every one should do) in a harsh, rough way, but, by coaxing and persuasion, get him to leave the place. When absolutely necessary to use force, or to call the aid of a policeman, do it at once, but never act like a brute. If a man is successful in this line of business, as I hope all may be who engage in it, he should refrain from having what is popularly known as a "swelled head." Success and failure alternate with each other, and boasting pride and bombastic demeanor should be left for the other fellow.

In order to meet with success, the "boss" must lay out his own hours of labor, and work as well within that time as any one of his employees do in their designated hours. He is a public servant, and must be governed by a rule of his own making, to have certain hours, which should never be neglected, and in which he *must attend* to his business. He will find that it is work, work, all the time, but the more you work, the more profit you will realize from the business.

Where there is a restaurant or hotel connected with the café, the proprietor should not, under any circumstances, allow himself to smoke. To one who is accustomed to do so, there should be some special time found, when he is away or off duty, to indulge in this habit. It also creates a bad impression, if the landlord or proprietor sits in his place, and accepts drinks from his friends or the customers. Sometimes the party, with whom he is sitting, drinks too much and becomes noisy. Therefore, as a rule, he should never engage in a social act of this kind. The guests will naturally judge the proprietor's character by the company he keeps. There is a proper time and place for drinking, and the place is always in the café or barroom. But it makes a bad impression upon the patrons of a café, where there are tables and chairs, to find the "boss" often sitting down with a party to drink champagne or any other wine. This action should be avoided entirely, if possible, for one reason, that when the proprietor is thus engaged, he must be neglecting, to some extent, his business. Furthermore, the other customers, who take only 10-cent or 15-cent drinks—men of moderate means—will feel slighted, and their feelings may possibly be hurt by seeing the proprietor too often engaged with these swell wine-drinking parties, and thus may come to the conclusion that he does not regard them or their patronage of any value.

There are very few proprietors who can do a sufficient business with parties "opening wine," in order to afford to neglect other customers. By so doing, he may drive away his best regular patrons. The daily 10-cent customer, as well as the occasional $5.00 guest, must be considered. The proper rule is, to avoid this drinking openly, in his own place, as much as possible. During the wine-drinking time, in addition to the loss of the correct supervision of his business, the proprietor hasn't the opportunity to give proper attention to his other customers, and may, therefore, offend some of them.

It will create the same bad feeling, in another instance, when a man, in a public business, goes out for sport, having a horse and carriage at his front-door, and the driver waiting, while the proprietor leaves his establishment with an attempt at grand style. Some of the customers, unable, at any time, to make such a display, will very probably remark in a satirical way:

"There goes my money!"—All such exhibitions should be kept away from the public eye, especially about a man's business establishment. It is not intended to say that a man should not take a ride, occasionally, with his family, or dress well when he pleases, but he should not make an ostentatious display of the means or luxury he may possess. If all this is avoided, the man can make money by not accepting champagne treats and by not driving about in swell rigs; but, instead of all this, by remaining in his place, and working hard to keep his patrons pleased, thereby gain more, and thus improve his financial standing.

24. KEEPING BOOKS IN A SIMPLE MANNER.

The keeping of books in a simple manner, by which you can, at a glance, see instantly the general statements relating to the progress of your business, with special review of details, is a necessity to us. The statements of this article are not made with the purpose of forming a contrast to general bookkeeping, as used in mercantile circles, because while that system is perfect, it is too intricate and enlarged for our use, and we need a more simplified form.

There should be one general book, a day (or entry) book, of the usual form, long and narrow, and as thick as you may desire, in which daily every entry of expense, or purchase, or anything connected with the business, is to be written, and at night the total sum footed up. Then, there are to be other small pass books (about 5 by 10 inches in size), one for the total daily expenses; one for the total cash receipts; one cash book each for the restaurant, bar, cigar stand, and rooms (if any); and one each—called a stock book—for the restaurant, bar, and cigar stand; and one book for your individual cash expenses. From your day book is to be transferred daily to your stock, cash, and expense books, all the items in it relating to the special departments, to the proper books. That is, every evening, or early the next morning, you enter from the day book the particular items belonging to the special stock books (the restaurant stock, the bar stock, etc.); the amount of cash received in the different departments in the different cash books (and all in the total cash book); and the expenses in the general expense book; footing up the amounts in all these different books. The sums expended for various purposes—of which you have an account in your day-book—should be added weekly, as should be also the sums in your various stock and cash books. You have then, by adding these various amounts in the separate books, every four or five weeks, at the end of every month a systematized statement of all expenditures and receipts, and of all stock taken in as well as of that which has been used. The amounts must tally with the sums total in all your books of daily entry, and these must tally with the sum daily—and also weekly and monthly—in the day book. You then have, at a glance, the difference between all your receipts and expenditures, and can tell, daily, weekly, or monthly, just how you stand in business. Your trial balance, to be drawn at the end of the month, will show whether you have made or lost money, and will give an opportunity to compare the items with previous ones, or with certain daily items.

Take an ordinary card-board, rule it off properly, and enter under different, written headings, of restaurant, bar, cigar, rooms, daily expense, etc., the cash receipts and cash expenditures (see plates on opposite pages), and you will not only have the difference between receipts and expenditures, but, dividing this difference by 26, or 30, or 31 (according to the number of working days in the month), you can obtain the average daily loss or profit. This card-board, which is virtually a trial-balance sheet, is continued in detail from month to month during the year, and at the end of twelve months you can obtain not only your average monthly profit or loss, but also the daily average as well. There is also possibly a need for an "extra-expense" book, as at many times the daily expenses are increased by extra and unusual expenses. During the Centennial Exposition of 1876, I had over 420 people working for me, in Philadelphia, and no bookkeeper; but, instead, used the method I have outlined here, and the stock company, which supervised the enterprise, was perfectly satisfied with my system. Again, it will only take from ten to fifteen minutes to make these various entries every day, and any one will find daily this brief period of time when there is nothing else to be done.

25. A RESTAURANT IN CONNECTION WITH A CAFÉ.

The café, in the American meaning of the word, is an improved bar-room; the latter term being the original and proper word. The name "café" has been adopted from European countries, and is now considered the more fashionable term. The difference, however, between a European café and an American bar-room is as great as that between day and night. The bar-room only exists in America, for the reason that the manner of business, circumstances, surroundings, the way of living here, native customs, all neces-

DAILY RECEIPTS
OF THE DIFFERENT DEPARTMENTS FOR ONE MONTH.

	TOTAL.	Bar.	Restaurant.	Rooms.	Cigars.
1	$348 85	$127 45	$140 20	$40 00	$41 20
2	371 15	137 75	165 10	30 00	38 30
3	334 25	136 70	127 40	35 00	35 15
4	383 70	148 25	160 35	45 00	30 10
5	376 85	143 75	160 05	40 00	33 05
6	338 60	145 25	125 20	30 00	38 15
7	449 65	170 25	197 40	35 00	47 00
8	298 60	110 10	120 25	37 00	31 25
9	428 13	139 25	197 85	40 00	51 05
10	365 60	124 30	155 30	48 00	38 00
11	313 45	135 05	106 30	30 00	42 10
12	385 70	155 25	150 40	43 00	37 05
13	373 35	145 20	156 30	37 00	34 85
14	429 70	173 80	175 40	41 00	39 50
15	320 65	102 15	140 50	35 00	43 00
16	376 50	136 25	150 00	39 00	51 25
17	400 95	162 85	155 05	45 00	38 05
18	394 35	151 60	170 20	40 00	32 55
19	389 80	140 50	160 30	48 00	41 00
20	385 30	155 35	157 80	40 00	32 15
21	478 25	190 45	202 95	45 00	39 85
22	356 30	120 15	155 05	39 00	42 10
23	379 25	157 35	150 10	41 00	30 80
24	361 75	138 25	158 50	29 00	36 00
25	399 85	157 30	156 40	47 00	39 15
26	399 10	151 40	172 95	34 00	40 75
27	366 15	138 40	157 50	33 00	37 25
28	420 80	190 50	150 20	45 00	35 10
29	394 25	130 10	177 10	46 00	41 05
30	368 45	136 20	151 05	38 00	43 20
Per Month	$11,389 30	$4,351 15	$4,703 15	$1,175 00	$1,160 00
Per Day	379 64	145 04	156 77	39 16	38 67

The above shows the Daily Receipts, which when added will give you the sum total for one month. It is then transferred to the monthly and yearly card or sheet.

This is my own devise which has always proved satisfactory in my business management.

This is a Yearly Trial Balance Sheet, which shows, from the different departments, the Entire Cash Receipts by the Year, Month and Day; as well as the Expenditures from the different departments in connection with Daily Expenses.

	Total Cash for 12 Months.	Bar Cash.	Bar Stock Paid.	Rest't Cash.	Rest't Stock Paid.	Cigars Cash.	Cigar Stock Paid.	Rooms Cash.	Daily Exp. Paid.	Net Profit per Month.
January	$11,389.30	$4,351.15	$2,005.50	$4,703.15	$2,900.00	$1,160.00	$750.00	$1,175.00	$3,700.00	$2,133.80
February	11,340.00	4,350.00	1,864.00	4,650.00	2,000.00	1,140.00	725.00	1,200.00	4,100.00	2,651.00
March	11,176.85	4,200.00	1,724.00	4,596.85	2,247.50	1,155.00	775.00	1,225.00	3,900.00	2,530.35
April	11,395.00	4,500.00	2,024.50	4,600.00	2,552.25	1,145.00	700.00	1,150.00	4,000.00	2,118.25
May	11,308.15	4,226.15	1,704.50	4,725.00	2,196.00	1,107.00	800.00	1,250.00	3,800.00	2,807.65
June	11,385.85	4,473.85	2,064.50	4,625.00	2,604.25	1,187.00	650.00	1,100.00	3,779.20	2,287.90
July	11,311.40	4,348.85	1,664.85	4,556.55	2,071.60	1,112.00	825.00	1,300.00	3,960.40	2,789.90
August	11,365.65	4,667.20	1,769.50	4,749.45	2,728.40	1,049.00	775.00	900.00	3,797.00	2,295.75
September	11,308.80	4,032.80	1,741.80	4,517.00	2,351.00	1,259.00	730.00	1,500.00	4,063.40	2,423.10
October	10,948.55	4,328.00	1,997.70	4,783.00	2,296.65	1,037.55	770.00	800.00	3,837.70	2,046.50
November	11,183.45	4,422.00	1,969.50	4,419.00	2,582.35	1,242.45	735.00	1,100.00	3,888.00	2,008.60
December	12,031.00	4,300.00	1,854.00	4,881.00	2,321.00	1,150.00	765.00	1,700.00	3,974.30	3,116.70
TOTAL Per Year	$136,144.00	$52,200.00	$22,383.50	$55,800.00	$28,751.00	$13,744.00	$9,000.00	$14,400.00	$46,800.00	$29,209.50
Per Month	1,345.33	4,350.00	1,865.29	4,650.00	2,395.91	1,145.33	750.00	1,200.00	3,900.00	2,434.13
Per Day	378.18	145.00	62.17	155.00	79.86	38.18	25.00	40.00	130.00	81.15

KITCHEN, BAR AND HOTEL EXPENSES.

DAILY KITCHEN EXPENSES.		DAILY BAR EXPENSES.		DAILY HOTEL EXPENSES.	
Wages, 18 people	$29 75	Wages, 7 people	$13 64	Wages, 5 people	$ 3 99
Rent	8 33	Rent	13 88	Rent	11 11
Meals, 18 people	7 20	Meals, 7 people	2 80	Meals, 5 people	2 00
Gas and electric light	2 00	Gas and electric light	1 00	Gas and electric light	3 50
Ice	2 00	Ice	1 50	Ice	50
Laundry	2 80	Laundry	50	Laundry	1 50
Breakage	2 00	Breakage	75	Breakage	50
Coal	1 50	Coal	50	Coal	1 00
Beer, 18 people	1 60	Beer, 7 people	1 00	Beer, 5 people	35
Lunch		Lunch	4 50	Lunch	
License		License	2 28	License	
Insurance	40	Insurance	40	Insurance	40
Water Tax	75	Water Tax	25	Water Tax	50
Extras, Alterations	1 50	Extras, Alterations	1 00	Extras, Alterations	1 00
Total	$59 65	Total	$44 00	Total	$26 35

The above tabulated form of the Daily Expenses is based in a supposed business where the rent is about $12,000 a year regarding that of the Café at $5,000 the Restaurant $3,000 and the Hotel $4,000; The expenses are based upon these supposed per cents ($\frac{5}{12}$, $\frac{3}{12}$, $\frac{4}{12}$) of rent for the different departments and divided up in proportion. The sum of the expenses of the 3 different departments aggregates $130.00 as given in the single table of Daily Expense.

DAILY EXPENSE.

Wages (for 30 employees)................	$47.20
Rent (rate at $12,000 a year)..............	33.32
Meals for the Help.......................	12.00
Gas and Electric Light...................	6.50
Ice	4.00
Laundry	4.80
Breakage	3.25
Coal	3.00
Beer for the Help.......................	2.95
Lunch	4.50
License	2.28
Insurance	1.20
Water Tax..............................	1.50
Alterations, Extras, Wear and Tear.........	3.50
	$130.00

The above shows the specified daily expense that is given in the amount of expense on the general yearly trial balance sheet.

PLATE No. 5.

CHAMPAGNE SOUR.　　BRANDY CRUSTA.

Copyrighted, 1888.

sitate, to some extent, the existence of what is known as a bar-room; a peculiar home institution, typical of the American people, which other countries could not and do not copy, foreign nationalities being so thoroughly dissimilar to the natives of the United States. Even in this great country where the conditions exist that have made the bar-room a popular institution, great changes have occurred of late years, and the bar-room has lost some of its characteristics, for the reason that the old-style American, who only cared to patronize it, has largely passed away, and the younger generation, trained to more general knowledge, has approved and adopted the customs of many other countries. The glory and the nature of the old-fashioned genuine American bar-room is, therefore, somewhat disappearing, and present-day establishments are drifting toward the scope of the European style, which consists of having a so-called café, in some slight imitation of the foreign namesake, always, more or less, in connection with a restaurant or a place to eat. This meets my approval, for I don't believe it to be beneficial to any man to drink too much, without having the stomach sustained with the proper food. A man is liable to be "toned up" by drink, during business hours, even with an empty stomach, when his constitution seems to demand a stimulant; but if his system is inherently weak, while one or two glasses of liquor may be correct, it would be wiser to regulate his habits by combining eating with his drinking. As every one knows, a glass of wine or of malt liquor, a cocktail, or a punch, in moderation, goes well with the meal, tones up the system, strengthens the weak nerves, and gives vigor to the entire body. There is a wrong way of doing many things;—one can drink too much water, eat too much or too little, which all results in breaking down one's health. There are excellent reasons for comparing a strictly drinking place with a bar-room (café) and a restaurant combined. For making money with little trouble the bar-room is to be preferred, for the reason that expenses are much less than those of a restaurant; the profits are larger; the public is much easier satisfied; the investment is smaller; the wear and tear as well as the general loss are less, and even the responsibility resting upon the proprietor is considerably less. A bar-room alone I consider play to manage, but every one is not fortunate enough in having the type of a successful, typical bar-room that was common in former years, for we are losing the charm of the old-time resort, and adopting, more and more, the methods and style of the Europeans.

For certain reasons, as previously mentioned, I advise people in our line of business, in case of necessity, to adapt themselves to the new demands and routine, no matter how hard it may be to take up the change of business, as it is better to bite into a sour apple at once, and accommodate themselves to the requirements of the present day.

If a man is compelled to make a change, or switch off from his original line, he must consider carefully, whether he is capable of managing the new venture, whether the locality is proper, and whether the neighborhood requires or demands it, as there is much more expense attached to the management of a restaurant than the ordinary person imagines.

In a bar-room only, an man can easily, if doing a large business, take in from $250 to $300 a day, and can run the place at a daily expense of about $60, the necessary chief help being from six to seven bartenders. As we figure in our line of business, the average receipts for every bartender, in a 10-cent house, is between $40 and $50. In a 15-cent establishment, the average would be between $60 and $70. In such a place there should be two cashiers—one for day-time and another for night-time—about two porters, one lunch-man; the wages of which, with the other expenses, such as rent, gas, ice, etc., in comparison, would run up to $60 a day. In showing these figures of expense, it is very easy for any one to ascertain, or reckon, what the profits will be. If a man is compelled to attach a restaurant to his café, he will find that the expenses are, proportionately, much greater. Suppose he takes in, on a daily average, $300, which is a fair restaurant trade, he would then require about one employe to every $10 or $12 of receipts. There would be necessary one chef, an assistant chef, a broiler cook, a vegetable cook, a night chef (when there are long hours), a butcher, possibly another assistant (entrée) cook, a coffee cook, two firemen, two engineers (one for day-time and another for night-time), four pot and dish washers, one silverware washer, all about the kitchen; a steward, a head-waiter, two captains (assistant head-waiters), ten waiters, two cashiers (one for day-time and another for night-time), two oystermen, and four omnibuses (men to help generally, carrying dishes, washing and cleaning windows and floors, brasswork and silverwork, which work should not be done by waiters). From this, which shows about how much help is required in a restaurant, the total expense of wages, including all running expenses, will be found to be, on an average, $115 a day. It is not specified that this is an exact sum in every place, as the rent and the wages paid to employees will necessarily vary in different establishments.

It requires a very good steward to be able to purchase food stuff at one-half, or 50 per cent., of the money that the receipts will bring in, that is, $150 in the business of $300 receipts. The sum expended by him will naturally vary, according to the season of the year. These combined sums, $115 + $150, equal to $265, leaving a profit of 35, or about ten per cent., daily. But take into consideration the breakage, unavoidable accidents, the interest on the sum invested, etc., and there is but little profit remaining. I know of hundreds of places whose profit does not average two per cent., and some even that are conducted at an actual loss, for the reason that some people in the restaurant business will not watch it carefully enough, do not work as hard as they ought, and have not the proper cheque system, in order to protect themselves from loss or leakages. From all this may be determined that it is not particularly easy to succeed in the restaurant business. These statements have been made by me, not to deter people from opening restaurants, because eating places are necessary; but in order to have every one consider what his capabilities and prospects are for success. There are localities where a person could not succeed in having a bar-room alone, when the community demands a restaurant, and if the proprietor has confidence in himself, he should start the business. It is true, that in some first-class establishments the profits appear large, because the prices are large; but, at the same time, the running expenses, and especially the "service," are also great, and the margin between the two is small. All this explains why I advise any one not to go into the restaurant business, if he can possibly help it. If you are doing sufficient business in the bar-room, and are making a fairly-sized good income, leave the restaurant alone. But there are points in its favor. If you must enter the business, provided you have the proper ability and knowledge, and are in a good neighborhood, you will secure a more respectable, reliable, higher-paying trade and a better reputation, and secure patronage sooner than with a bar-room alone, for the general reason that people everywhere are always making inquiry for the place where a good table is set. Therefore, it is advisable for a man to secure one of the best chefs as well as assistant cooks, while all the kitchen employees must be thoroughly capable and of benefit to him, by preventing wastefulness and injury. There should be a thoroughly reliable steward (if the services of one are required), and the head-waiter and all the assistants should be, especially, capable men. The proprietor should be thoroughly convinced that he is dealing only with the best butchers, vegetable men, grocers, bakers, etc., when starting his restaurant; make a careful selection of the proper help, and then, as the great, important point, have the kitchen fitted up in perfect convenience, perfect handiness, and in the latest style, with all the most-approved appliances, as money should not be spared in fitting up a dining-room or kitchen. The latter, if possible, must be well and conveniently located, properly lighted and ventilated, of sufficient size, of good height to the ceiling, located on the main floor, if possible, over a basement that is also thoroughly ventilated. First of all, have a proper place for the ice-box; meat-box; fish-box; oyster-box; butter, egg, and milk box; vegetable box, and all others that are necessary. It is wise to have a good, substantial range of sufficiently large size, broilers (hard and charcoal), a practical steam-table, a place for hot water, coffee and tea urns or kettles, a comfortable dish-warmer or heater, an extra little ice-box (convenient for the fancy dishes of the chef), the proper protection or some form of hut over the range, and a convenient rack for placing pans, etc. (one, however, that will not obstruct the view of the kitchen). Then, there should be water tanks of proper size for washing your pots (castrols) and dishes (one for hot, and the other for cold water), and enough shelving to place your utensils upon. It is also important to have an elevated table or stand fitted up, which, to be conveniently arranged, should be placed near, or in the vicinity of, the steamtable for the special purpose of having the different dishes in better view. The flooring of the place, especially near the range, should properly be of bricks or asphalt. With a wooden floor, it is liable to get greasy, full of stains, becomes slippery, and, necessarily, looks badly. The bricks can be easily scrubbed and rubbed clean.

In fixing up the kitchen have it very convenient for the cooks to place the castrols near the range, to do away with unnecessary walking, making it more agreeable for the cooks. The pot-washer should also have a shelf, upon which to place his soap, cans, brushes, etc. The edge of the water-boxes should be lined with metal (soft lead, for instance), in order to avoid the wearing out of the boxes, and to keep the pots from being dented. There should be kept ready for use pot-brushes, soap, sapolio, rags, etc., for cleaning copper-ware as well as the sinks. A table should also be placed in the kitchen—when there isn't room in the restaurant—for the convenience of fixing and dressing the necessary salads (lobster, potato, chicken, etc.), for the silverware, butter plates, bread plates, cut bottles, tub with cracked ice, pitchers for dressing, etc. It is a very practical point to have your stationary boxes, such as water-boxes for washing dishes, connected in such a way, as to have hot water in one box, cold water in the one adjoining, and a third box, if possible, in which to place the crockery, that has been washed, out of hand. Wherever the boxes for the dish-washer may be placed, it is absolutely necessary to have a sufficient amount of shelving, upon which to place tools, but not too many shelves, for they are liable to accumulate dirt, filth, roaches, and other insects; and, wherever the water-boxes and steam-table are located, the floor should be kept in a very dry and clean condition. The fact is, that the floor of the entire kitchen should be kept in such a perfect condition, without slops or grease, that it could be subjected to inspection at any time. It should be the leading advertisement in the hotel and restaurant—the pride of both, the proprietor and the employees there.

All the necessary ice-boxes should be constructed in such a way (the door not too large or inconvenient), that not too much cold air can escape or warm air enter. The most practical ice or order-box is one made with drawers having a certain number each for steaks, chops (mutton or lamb), etc., for, by having them constructed very particularly and close, they have many special advantages. With the drawers there is no necessity for opening the door, allowing the temperature to be lowered, the melting of ice, etc.

There should be two chopping blocks; one for fish, lobsters, turtles, etc.; and another for meats only. It is wise to have, if possible, the restaurant room separated from the café by a partition, if nothing more, with a communicating door, convenient for guests as well as waiters. The restaurant proper should look charmingly and cheerfully, and, yet, be thoroughly practical and adapted to the needs of business; good light and ventilation being absolutely necessary. Lately it has been customary to have an elegant carpet on the floor, the tables and chairs more or less handsome, according to the proprietor's taste, and no matter how rich in texture the furnishings are, they should not be gaudy, as it is difficult to keep them clean. Knives, forks, spoons, carving knives should be of the best material, the silverware substantial and tasteful, and the crockery-ware, plates and cups of the finest quality. There should be good cabinet work for the decoration of the room, mirrors and looking-glasses, if desirable, as they generally are, hat and coat stands and racks, electric fans in the summer time, handsome pot plants and flowers, and some handsome paintings—all of which add to the beauty of the apartment. Good linen-ware, table-cloths, napkins, etc., are also necessary. The keeping of everything clean and dusted is perfectly apparent. Fresh, clean bills of fare should not be forgotten. Everything of the finest quality is needed for a first-class place.

As a rule, the management, the service, and keeping the place in order is the head-waiter's duty, who also sees that every patron gets the proper atttention. One particular point is, that the man in charge of the dining room should know that every customer receives the same kind of service, whether he tips the waiter or not. It is a great mistake to allow any neglect of regular patrons. As far as I am concerned, I claim that the people who do not give tips should be treated just as well as those who do. It is nothing to the proprietor in a financial way, but only an evidence of good will by those who desire to acknowledge their appreciation of the waiter's efforts. Many restaurant and hotel proprietors have lost patrons, because the latter were slighted by the waiters, but did not care to complain and simply withdrew their custom. It is the proprietor's duty to see that such an incident does not occur in his place. No one opens a place for the purpose of having waiters receive tips, but for selling goods offered. I do not object to waiters receiving tips, and the man, who gives one, is mostly benefited, because the waiter will give him more attention and pleasant service. The fact is, that writers of almost all the nations in the world have argued and written many articles on the subject, denouncing the custom of giving and receiving tips, but there will never be any change, for the reason, principally, that there is not enough clear money—profit—in the restaurant business to allow paying the waiters and other employees good living wages. The expenses are so enormous that the proprietor is obliged to hire men for the lowest possible wages, at which he can get them. If he were to pay his men fair wages—from $12 to $15 a week—he would be obliged to charge much more, and have, altogether, a higher-priced bill of fare. Numbers of people would not then be able to patronize restaurants, who are in the habit of doing so now. This is the reason why the waiter receives tips, as his wages are generally not sufficient to pay his living expenses. It is not always the meanness or parsimony of the proprietors, but forced circumstances that compel them to pay their help small wages. Give the owner or manager of an establishment more profit and, generally, he would cheerfully advance the wages of his waiters and other assistants.

There are thousands of waiters who would rather not receive tips, if they could demand and receive the proper wages that would support them and their families. There are as many men in this line of business who have just as good a character and principles as men in any other endeavor to earn a living; but the vocation makes a man slavish, and he is virtually compelled to accept presents (tips) from generously inclined people, in order to get money enough to pay his own expenses.

Another point, to which my attention has been drawn hundreds of times, is, that waiters when cleaning off a table, just after a party has left, are in the habit of beating the cloth with their napkins and whipping off the crumbs, which may possibly drop upon people sitting at an adjoining table. This is entirely wrong. The crumbs should be brushed off carefully into a crumb pan, or mopped up with the napkin, so that the guests in the vicinity may not be disturbed.

I do not wish it to be understood that every feature of the restaurant and café has been mentioned by me, but only some of the principal points specified, as it would take too much time and voluminous space to itemize everything, connected with the subject.

— 94 —

My simple purpose has been to present a clear view of the leading principles in connection with the restaurant principally, and not to enter into a thousand details, many of which will be readily learned by experience in business.

26. IN CONNECTION WITH THE CHECK SYSTEM.

At present, in every well-regulated bar-room, restaurant, and hotel, there should be a perfectly devised check system. In a café, there is needed a cash register, and where there is a number of bartenders working, each one should have his own register, in order to have an account of his individual sales every day. In a large establishment, where there is much business done, I have found it most convenient, during my years of experience, to have a cashier, in addition to the cash registers. The reason why I approve of a check system is, because it is then much easier for the bartender to attend to his duty without interference. For example, where there is a cash register and no cashier, and the bartender is obliged to ring up his check as well as make change, hand the balance to the customer, etc., it interferes with his work, especially in a "rush," is very annoying, and is likely to cause the bartender to make a mistake. No one knows better than myself the difficulties of a multiplicity of duties when there is a large crowd hurrying the bartender to wait upon them, take their orders and hand back the change. The most practical system is the one by which you turn out the amount, whatever it may be, on a printed check, and after it comes out from this Krause machine, it is the bartender's duty to put the check in front of the customer from whom he receives the money, handing both money and check to the cashier. Otherwise, where there is no cashier, the cash registers are the best—one for each bartender. In a restaurant attached to the café or bar-room, I found the most practical system to be as follows: Each waiter should have two check books, one for the restaurant and one for the kitchen, each bearing the number (name or letter) by which he is known, 1, 2, 3 or 4, etc., for instance, one of the books (preferably the restaurant one) being made of white paper and the other of a different color, such as yellow or brown.

Both check books should each have at the head of each page the printed name and address of the proprietor, with the name of the kind of check, the waiter's number in one corner and the check number in the other (the latter running from 1 to 100, for instance), all inscribed on a stub, below which is a perforated line, and under that, again, the printed number of the waiter and of the check. The printed numbers of the check orders will run in rotation, No. 1 on page 1, No. 2 on page 2, etc., always corresponding with the number on the stub above, the printed matter, otherwise being the same on each and every page of the books. The filled page of the order, filled out by the waiter, below the stub is to be torn off as used.

Upon the page of the yellow paper book, the waiter pencils the entire order as given by the customer or party being served. Then, going to the kitchen, he sings out the order, or, if there is a checker (or stamper) there, then the latter calls out the order and stamps the check—separated from the stub of the book—which is then placed by the waiter or checker in a pigeon-hole, in a properly arranged shelf, which the chef or checker has under his charge, each pigeon-hole being numbered 1, 2, 3, etc., to correspond with the number of the waiter. These pigeon-holes should be built in a row. as are ordinarily fixed in a counting room, but each with a slant backwards, so that the waiter will not have the opportunity to take out again the check for the purpose of correction or any other reason; while, at the same time, the checks can easily be taken out by the chef or checker on the other side. If there is any dispute between the waiter and cooks regarding the order, the chef or checker has possession of that order, which shows exactly what was asked for and stops argument at once. The prices are placed on the order (or kitchen) check and must agree, in sum and totals, with the same amount written by the same waiter or his white paper check, which is handed to the customer at the proper time.

The cashier in a restaurant should have, properly, a set of files, consecutively numbered, upon which to place the correspondingly numbered waiter's cash checks, which are handed him by either waiter or customer. At the end of the day's business the cashier makes up the sum totals of each waiter's checks, and the complete sums of all the checks must agree with all the sums of the yellow paper checks, individually and combined, in the possession of the chef or checker in the kitchen. If there is a difference, it must be explained, usually by deducting the sum in dispute from the waiter's wages. There is no way of making a mistake or danger of loss to the management if this system is used, and though it may be troublesome to both waiters and chef or checker, it is absolutely necessary to secure an accurate report of each day's business, the sum of the various checks agreeing with the sum against each waiter's account (as made out by himself in both the white paper and the yellow paper checks) and the amount of money in the cash drawer.

If it should happen, as is liable, that a mistake has occurred by the waiter making out a cash check of a larger amount than his kitchen check, which would naturally entail a loss upon him and thereby benefit

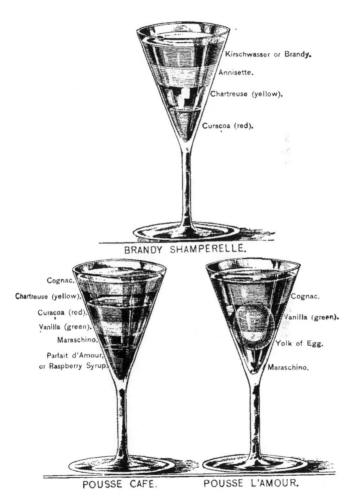

the restaurant, the management should allow the waiter to explain and give him just treatment. The opportunity should be given him, in the presence of the cashier or manager, to compare both checks, the number as well as the amounts, so that every waiter will have his just rights as much as the proprietor. I don't mean to say that every one should adopt my system, nor do I try to impress upon any one the absolute necessity of following it, to be successful; but, after the trial of many systems, in different cities, I have found to my own satisfaction that this is the best and most reliable for my purpose.

When a waiter has an order for any drink, it is then his duty to go to the cashier and state the order, and then the cashier, who has entire charge of the bar pads, writes out the order on the waiter's checks, which are numbered the same as others. With the order, the waiter will then call for the drinks at the bar, and give his check to the cashier or to the man who attends to that department. The waiter should then put all these items on the cash check, which must tally in amount with the other checks—kitchen and bar.

27. CONCERNING THE HIGH-PROOF OF LIQUORS, WHISKIES, BRANDIES, ETC.

Years ago, before anything was known about blended goods, it was every man's business in our line to know thoroughly how to reduce high-proof goods to the proper proof required by the public, or what they considered fit to drink. Then, all first-class bartenders had to understand not alone the art of mixing drinks, but to reduce (or cut) the high-proof goods, blend them and fix them up, properly, so they would give satisfaction to the customers. Those days have passed, and the present method is much more convenient, the goods now manufactured and distilled being much more uniform and giving better satisfaction.

One ordering goods from a distillery now can have his own blend, as he orders, according to the desires and tastes of his customers, and also the proper proof of all his whiskeys, as all these will be properly and satisfactorily distilled and blended without any further trouble to the proprietor. Whiskeys, as a rule, are now sold at an average of from 93 to 95 proof. This varies, of course, to some extent, and what is required all depends on the class of trade that the proprietor has.

As far as imported goods, gins, rums, brandies, etc., are concerned, they all, more or less, come over-proof, and therefore it is advisable to reduce them to about 100, for by selling it over-proof, the proprietor would not be able to have returned the amount of money invested. It is difficult, anyway, to make a profit on imported goods.

In buying bonded (or imported) goods, it is well for the purchaser to select, of course, a first-class firm who handles the best grade of liquors, always being sure to get an order from the importers on their bonded warehouse, to have the goods delivered to you. By this means you know the liquors have not been adulterated, as is possibly the case when they have been removed first to the cellars or warehouse of the importer. When it requires a reduction of the imported liquors, as they come generally from 12 to 15 over-proof, the proper amount of water required for this reduction will be one pint to a gallon of the liquor, in order to bring the proof from 115 to 100, the usual retail sale proof of imported liquors. They are generally drank stronger than the domestic goods, because they are still further diluted when served, as they usually are, in hot (water) drinks.

I do not mean to say that any first-class importing house adulterates their liquors, as this is only done by those who have no reputation at stake, and who take the opportunity of doing so when the liquors are in their own warehouses, before being sold to the retailer.

28. SOME REMARKS ABOUT MORTGAGES.

It has been the custom of late in places fixed up as bar-rooms, cafés, restaurants, etc., where large sums of money are involved, in order to have the arrangements, fixtures and furnishings fashionable, costly and up to date for the style of our business, has changed according to the dictates of fashion—to place a mortgage as security for money advanced, when there has not been sufficient capital to pay for the entire outlay. It has even been done by those who had the money, but did not care to invest the entire sum in a new enterprise. Heretofore, a person starting with a moderate capital, in an ordinary place, has been able to do a good, successful business; but times have changed, and with few exceptions no one is able longer to do so. Anyone expecting to be very successful in our line of business must fix up his establishment in the latest style, and as it requires quite an amount of capital to do so, there are many instances where the proprietor has not sufficient cash and is obliged to place a mortgage upon the place.

The drawback upon having the mortgage is that you must pay yearly interest upon it and will never feel fully satisfied that you are the proprietor or "boss." Again, the people, such as brewers or wholesale liquor dealers, who generally hold the mortgage, do not consider you a good business customer for this reason, and will not give you the same attention as they do others who are not indebted to them. Of course, a first-class, honorable concern will not take advantage of your situation or make any distinction in their treatment of you from other buyers, but some will do so and imagine that almost any class of supplies is good enough for the customers of a mortgaged place. This is one side of the question, a bad feature, necessarily, and one that will be detrimental to your business. On the other hand, it is something of a benefit to have your place mortgaged, for in case you should be disposed to sell the place, you may then more easily find a customer to buy, as many would be more readily satisfied when it did not take so much cash to complete the financial transaction.

For instance, a business representing the value of $50,000 or $100,000 is frequently very difficult to dispose of, it being seldom that any buyer or investor is willing to risk such a large sum, no matter how good the business may be; but where there is a mortgage of from $25,000 to $50,000 or a similar proportion on the price asked, it is easier to sell in a more satisfactory manner, especially if the mortgage is held by an honorable party. In consideration of these facts, therefore, I would advise any person in taking a place at such a great cost as $50,000 or more, where there is so much risk, to buy it with a good-sized mortgage, or know that they will be able to secure one when purchasing, as it will relieve him of the fear of losing as much—in case there should be a failure—as he would otherwise.

Where the investment requires a large sum and where it is the intention of the buyer to take up a mortgage, it is then best for him to see that he secures as long a lease as possible, with a reasonable rent, for the principal reason that no responsible firm, such as a brewer or wholesale liquor dealer, would take the risk and accept the inducement, unless this is done, to advance the amount of money required.

If a man succeeds in getting a good-sized mortgage on his place, he will be benefited, because in selling the place he would receive a larger price, proportionately, as the purchaser seldom takes into consideration the amount of the mortgage, and would the more readily find a cash buyer. There are other instances also when it is beneficial to have a mortgage, such as illness or death, when it would become necessary to close out the business at short notice, and, even under compulsion, the mortgaged place would sell better. This is, of course, where one individual owns the place, with simply his own money invested. With a stock company it would necessarily be different. They would not probably allow a mortgage to remain upon the place. But it must be apparent to every one that a mortgage is not necessarily detrimental but, on the contrary, may be of benefit. All this is merely a statement of opinion, people being left to act upon their own judgment. If dealing with a good, reliable concern, holding a mortgage upon your place, and you are known to be a respectable, hard-working business man, you will never be pressed by them, nor will they act against your interests, because it would be injurious to their own.

Naturally, where there is a mortgage it should be recorded, as the law requires, and the owner or holder should see that it is renewed annually—this relates to movable fixtures. From all this you may come to the conclusion what is best for you to do.

29. A FEW REMARKS ABOUT CASHING CHECKS.

At the present time (and for several years past) it is a custom for the general public to have their drafts or checks, or both, cashed in hotels, restaurants and saloons—in some places more than in others—as a convenience to themselves.

It is well for every one in business life, if he can avoid cashing checks, to do so, for he will thereby escape much annoyance. By cashing checks, the proprietor, in all cases, takes more or less risk, for a check is never real money but only a promissory note.

Where one is compelled to give the public accommodation, more or less, he can never be too careful in considering what he is doing. First of all, he should know the party who asks the favor, his standing financially and socially. If the man is a comparative stranger, he should know all about the maker of the check, his business place, his private address, and his responsibility. The proprietor should carefully examine the check and see whether the date is made ahead or not, as, in the former case, it is considered a matter of trust. Notice that the check is properly made out, with correct signature, and see whether it is payable at the local city bank or at some out-of-town bank. When collected from some other than the home bank, there is usually a slight expense of collection. It is to be remembered also that at present—for the purpose of a war tax—a two-cent revenue stamp must be attached to every check, the stamp cancelled by writing the date and initials of the "maker" upon it.

When a person presents a check of which he is not the maker, the utmost carefulness must then be observed for several reasons. Whether you know the maker or not, you must be informed of his business and home address, and what probable responsibility he has. If you know all about the endorser, that he is a man of good standing and ample means, and the check is afterward returned to you, marked "N. G." or stamped "Insufficient Funds," then you have an opportunity to collect by process of law, if necessary, from the endorser. To repeat: In every case you should know the business and residence address of all those connected with the check—the maker, the endorser, and the person who presents the check.

Another point is, that when you accommodate your patrons by cashing their checks, and a certain party is in the habit of taking advantage of your willingness very often, it is then wise to find out the reason why, for, as a rule, a man that makes it a habitual practice of using checks in payment is one who has not much money in the bank, and this class generally exist and keep up their bank account on the strength of other people's money. For instance: There are a set of men known as "check writers"—you may know them by their over-politeness and frequently their extreme generosity, which costs them nothing—who may have in bank the sum of $5, $2, or only five cents. Cashing a check of $200 with you, they will deposit $150, keep the balance in their pocket, and, during the same day or upon the next, will cash another check for $100 or more elsewhere, deposit enough of this to make the check you have taken "good," and in all probability will be asking the same favor of you again in a few days and repeat it from time to time with you, and probably several other people, always increasing the size of the sum of money, until at last they are finally refused everywhere, and then the crash comes. They are then, as they have always virtually been, bankrupt, and you and others must lose the amount of the last check cashed. It is useless to sue them, and you have no chance for criminal prosecution against them, because they have always had an account at the bank.

If I had any advice to give, it would be not to cash any checks whatever, if it is possible to avoid doing so. Where there is a large number of checks cashed, there will be some trouble, if not actual loss, connected with the collections. In cashing checks, you should also have your wits about you, be as calm and collected as a bank official, examine the check, back and front, and see that it is perfectly drawn. Do not keep checks in your possession a minute longer than possible, but immediately place them in your bank, with your endorsement, for collection. By neglecting to do so, you may lose from no other reason than the failure of the parties drawing the checks or the banks upon which they are drawn, for if you do not deposit at once the law holds that you gave the maker a stipulated time, and you will not have the benefit of an ordinary claim against your debtors.

Another important point is the common but exceedingly wrong habit of letting customers have blank checks. It is best not to do so under any circumstances unless you know perfectly well the one asking the favor of you, because this is how the rogue gets an opportunity to forge both the body and signature of a check, having the right form and knowing where the party he intends to defraud deposits. I do not pretend to know all about banking formulas and arrangements, but I have had experience with checks, because in one place kept by me there were $5,000,000 worth passed through my hands in the course of a number of years.

It is also well, in our line of business, to decline to lend cash money to customers, no matter whether an I. O. U., a due bill, or security, such as a watch, diamonds, etc., are offered. If a man wants to lose his trade, all he has to do is to loan some of his customers cash, and then he need not wonder why they remain away, though some of his other patrons may. It is not alone the sum of money you may lose, but also the trade, friendship, and even good will of the man you have accommodated, for, in giving reason why he does no longer patronize your place, he may talk injuriously against you and your business. This will happen in nine cases out of ten.

Even in case of a certified check, which is generally considered to be equivalent of cash, there is possibly a chance that the certification may be a forgery, and if you are not perfectly well acquainted with the personages or the standing of the maker you should refuse it in all cases. People having places in the upper part of New York City must, necessarily, be more cautious than those down town, because the proprietors of places in the southern section are nearer the banking centre and usually know thoroughly the general standing and reputation of those who would place checks with them.

In some establishments, it is even wise to put up a printed notice, reading: "Absolutely no checks cashed here," and if the proprietor can keep that rule unbroken it will be all the better for him.

30. RULES IN REFERENCE TO A "GIGGER."

In all my recipes for the various drinks, you will find the term "wine glass" indicating the article to be used in which to mix drinks. The wine glass is only used for compiling these recipes; but for measuring the mixture, etc., the proper article to be used is what is called a "gigger," otherwise considerable liquor would be wasted in case of a rush of business. The use of the "gigger" also enables one to get the drinks at once the way the customers desire to have them, either strong or medium, for there is no man in the business who can pour out of a bottle a certain quantity of liquor by guessing at it, especially when the bottles used are only half filled or nearly empty.

The "gigger" is of silver-plated metal, and is shaped like a sherry glass without the long stem. It is durable and almost impossible to break, and is used by all first-class bartenders, except only a few experts in the art of mixing drinks who have had such experience and practice that they can measure accurately by eyesight alone, without even using a glass for measuring.

31 A FEW WORDS REGARDING LAGER BEER.

Lager beer (or bier) is so well known in this country as well as in all parts of the world that only a few remarks are necessary concerning it. But it requires the same attention as all other liquors or beverages, and even more than some of them. It depends entirely on the manner of handling it whether beer has a cool, refreshing taste or not. It should always be kept at an even temperature, according to the atmosphere and season of the year—in summer at an extreme temperature of from 40 to 45 degrees—and in the ice house at least three or four days before the keg or barrel is tapped. I would, therefore, advise any one intending to sell lager in his place not to spare the expense of having an A No. 1 ice box or ice house, which should always be kept in good working condition by being filled with ice sufficient to obtain the desired temperature at all seasons of the year. Have the ice depository large enough for the demands of your business and you will not have trouble in supplying your customers with good lager beer.

32. HOW LAGER BEER SHOULD BE DRAWN AND SERVED.

The proper way to draw lager is directly from the keg, not using the first one or two glasses, until the beer runs freely; then the vent must be knocked into the bung. If lager is drawn through pipes, they should be of the best material—properly, English block tin—and be kept perfectly clean and in good order. It is customary to have a carbonated water or air pressure constantly acting upon the beer when it is drawn through the pipes to prevent it from getting flat or stale, and impart a fresh and pleasant taste to the beer. But proper attention must be given to keeping the boiler containing the air in a very clean condition, and if the boiler stands in a place where the air is impure, it is advisable to connect the boiler and pump by means of a pipe to some outlet where perfectly fresh air is obtainable. Foul air will give the beer a bad taste and probably sicken the people drinking it. The beer remaining in the pipes over night should not be used. Attention must be given to prevent the pressure on the beer from being too high, as this would keep the lager from running freely, and by converting it into froth or cream, make it unhandy for the bartender to draw. There is also danger of an explosion if the pressure becomes very high, and this is liable to destroy the beer kegs, pipes or rubber hose connections with the boiler. An explosion is more likely to occur at night than during the day.

Before drawing the beverage, the bartender should see that the glasses are perfectly clean. After filling them, remove the superfluous froth with a little ruler, for by so doing you will prevent a great amount of moisture from spreading over the counter and floor, the foam in the glass will remain firm longer, and the beer will thus be prevented from getting flat quickly. By not removing the loose froth the air bubbles on top will sink through the froth and dissolve it.

When a customer orders a second glass of beer, the same glass should be used without previous rinsing, because the beer will both look and taste better. If a party of two or more are standing up at the bar and a second "round' is called for, it is proper to take the same glasses, one by one at a time, and refill them, and not two or three at a time, as many bartenders do, for they are likely to mix them, an incident that would be unpleasant to customers. Handling the classes carefully is pleasing to them, and should be done, if the bartender has sufficient time to do it, but in case of "a rush," put aside the glasses used in the first place and let your customers see that you have taken fresh glasses. The same rule should be observed in serving customers sitting around a table. All these suggestions are of importance. Remember to have your beer always cold enough in summer and of the right temperature in winter. I, moreover, advise any one not to use air pressure if it can possibly be helped, as the beer will always have a bad after-taste and it always loses a part of the real flavor. In using the carbonated pressure, it is more expensive, but it is best not to avoid this item of expense, for the beer is kept fresher, the foam is always bubbling, and the customers are therefore fully satisfied. If your cylinder as well as the pipes are in good condition, as they both ought to be, one cylinder will be enough to force from twenty to thirty half-barrels of beer. The cylinder is usually sold at a very reasonable price.

PLATE No. 7.

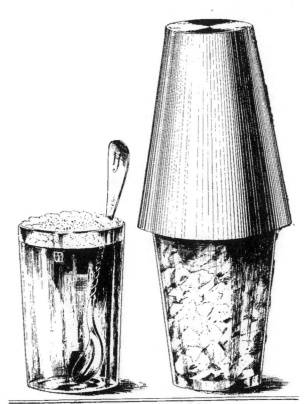

MORNING GLORY FIZZ.

Copyrighted, 1888.

33. ABOUT BOTTLED LAGER BEER.
(Imported as well as Domestic.)

With bottled lager, the method is altogether different. It must not be kept on ice, but in a very cool place in the ice box, in an upright position, to allow the sediment to settle. In pouring the beer from the bottles, it is the bartender's or waiter's duty to select a proper and clean glass. All this applies with equal force to both imported and domestic beers. At the present time bottled beer has become quite the fashion, and is consumed much more than in former years, especially in hotels, restaurants and private families. The proprietor of any place should buy all the best brands of bottled beer, as the customer of to-day demands quality and variety. In stocking up, you must see that not too great a quantity or too much of any single brand is taken at one time, because the older bottled beer gets, the more it loses its flavor, unless it is the special brewed beer of the export trade. Bottled beer should never be kept more than from two to three weeks in the ice box, and in handling it it is proper to try to dispose first of the oldest lot on hand, in order to keep the quantity uniform. In opening the bottle, the bartender should be careful in pulling the cork and brush away any particles of it with a clean towel. Furthermore, bottled beer should be handled as carefully as wine and not in the careless, slipshod manner so many bartenders use.

34. ABOUT CLEANING BEER AND ALE PIPES.

At present nearly every saloon having lager beer, ale or porter (so-called malt liquors) on tap, is supplied with an apparatus, the boiler, pipes, rubber hose and other attachments to it, which should be kept perfectly clean. This will be easy to accomplish in the following manner: If a barrel of beer or ale is emptied, and it is found necessary to cleanse the pipes, take a pail or two of hot water and stir into it about half a pound of washing soda. Put this fluid into the empty barrel, attach the vent and put on the pressure. Then turn on the faucet and let it take its own course, the same as beer, and it will be forced through the pipes. When it is seen that the barrel is emptied, take out the vent and pour in a few pailfuls of clean water; then close the vent and again put on the pressure to force the clean water through the pipes. In this way all the pipes and connections can easily and perfectly be cleaned, will have a fresh smell, and you are certain of having good beer. A necessary cleaning should be made once or twice a week according to the amount of business done.

35. RELATING TO PUNCH BOWLS.

It is of importance to know how to properly cool punches. To do it correctly, take a metal dish of sufficient size to hold the bowl containing the punch, put the bowl inside of this and completely fill the space between the bowl and dish with finely shaved ice on which a little rock salt is sprinkled to prevent it from melting quickly. In letting the ice reach over the rim of the bowl and having a few leaves spread over it, or otherwise ornamented, the bartender can produce a fine effect and always have made a cool and refreshing punch. Decorating the outside of the dish by having a bright colored napkin or towel around it, place punch glasses around the bowl, and the **whole arrangement will look especially inviting.**

36. THE PROPER STYLE IN OPENING AND SERVING CHAMPAGNES.

In serving champagne, the bartender, after being informed which brand the customer requires, places the champagne glass before him, takes the bottle from the ice, twists or cuts off the wire, and then cuts the string by which the cork is held in place just below the neck of the bottle; if cut otherwise, parts of the string, with some of the sealing wax attached to it, will remain fastened to the bottle, and particles of wax are liable to drop into the glass while the wine is being poured out. After the cork is removed, the mouth and neck of the bottle should be wiped off with a clean towel or napkin.

When a party of gentlemen enter your place and champagne is called for, as a matter of politeness, first pour a few drops into the glass of the gentleman who called for the wine, then fill the glasses of those he invited, before completely filling his glass. This rule of etiquette should be observed in serving any wine, whether champagne or not. If a party at a table calls for champagne, place the bottle in an ice-cooler; it is also not proper to uncork the bottle previous to placing it upon the table before the guests. If frozen champagne, which is often called for, is desired, place the bottle in the ice-cooler and then fill up the cooler with broken ice and rock salt to the top. Revolve the bottle backward and forward with both hands as rapidly as possible; then cut the string and draw the cork and place a clean napkin over the mouth of the bottle. You will find that the wine will freeze much quicker in this way than if the cork is left in the bottle. This is what is called frozen wine or champagne frappé.

In a place where there is a great demand for champagne and many cases of it sold, it is advisable to have an extra ice box made—which may be called "a champagne box"—to contain that special brand of wine. Champagne should be as near the freezing point as possible, but when placed in the general box—used for all purposes, and which is continually being opened—it will never be sufficiently cold and will, therefore, fail to give satisfaction. For the investment that it will take to pay for an extra champagne box, the recompense will come in the saving of ice, the cost of which amounts to a considerable sum during the year. This box will be opened only occasionally, will be less expensive than the use of a general box, and last longer, while it requires only two pails of broken ice daily, and, if necessary, a little rock salt. By the use of this box you not only keep the wine and labels in good condition, but secure the full satisfaction of your customers. The wine also retains its flavor because of the constant steady temperature.

37. PURCHASING SUPPLIES.

In buying and laying in your goods, it is advisable to consider well and carefully with whom you are going to deal. Friendship in business has its variations. Your best friends in the wholesale trade may not have the line of goods you desire, and there are cases even when it is preferable for you to maintain business relations only with those who are comparative strangers. Of course, your friends may have the best goods, and it would then be foolish for you to trade elsewhere. Ordinarily, you should go to those who have an established reputation and are known to handle only first-class goods and of every kind required. It is not altogether advisable to deal entirely with those people you imagine spend the most money in your place for the purpose of obtaining orders from you, because, in nine cases out of ten, you are really obliged to pay back more in higher prices for your goods than they have spent with you. It is perfectly natural for every man to try and make a profit and to recover, in some form, his expenditures. The spending of money or treating by wholesale people in our line of business should never be considered as a possible profitable connection, as long as you are sure you get the proper goods you require—first class and at the lowest price. Furthermore, it is best to deal with parties who have the agencies of the best goods in the market.

It is always preferable to purchase your stock on cash terms, which is either spot cash or ten days' time, because you then get the best discount which amounts to a considerable sum in the course of a year and adds handsomely to your profits. For example: where there is a business of $50,000 per annum, the discount of from five to ten per cent. would alone be a sufficient profit for some small business places. In paying cash for your goods you will be benefited everywhere. Those people with whom you deal will take better care of your orders, have more respect for you, while at the same time you are more independent. All this enhances your general reputation as a proprietor and a man of business affairs. On the contrary, by getting goods on credit and allowing people to wait a long time for their money, those selling to you will not be personally interested in you, will not be as particular in making up your orders and, possibly, push upon you an inferior grade of goods. Under every circumstance it should be understood that any one in our line of business should pay cash, because he sells for cash, and generally receives this money before his bills are due to the wholesale dealer. You will find that it pays best in the long run to sell a good article at a fair profit.

38. HANDING BAR-SPOONS TO CUSTOMERS.

In serving drinks it is proper to give a short-handled bar-spoon with them, so that the customer, if he desires, may take out some of the fruit, such as a slice of orange or pineapple, a strawberry, cherries or olives, and can do so without putting his finger into the glass. Gentlemen often find it inconvenient to remove their gloves while drinking, therefore a bar-spoon should be given with any mixed drink containing fruit. Bartenders should be very careful to see that in every drink they mix there is no uncleanliness, and the glass they strain the drink into should be as dry as possible. Furthermore, a small fancy napkin should be placed alongside the drink in order to benefit the customer.

39. HOW TO KEEP CELLAR AND STORE-ROOM.

The especial point in the arrangement of a cellar is to have it laid out properly for the different departments. That for ales and porters on draught should be very convenient and large enough to contain the skids on which the malt liquors are to be placed. Also a little extra platform, on which Bass' Ale should be placed standing, though the other brands must be placed in a horizontal position. Bass' Ale must be kept separate, because it requires the greatest of care. Where there is the slightest shaking, it will become upset, and will require from two to ten days to get back to its previous proper condition. Bass' Ale as well as other malt liquors should be drawn from pipes—as previously mentioned—of the very best material, and, if possible, located near the bar or counter.

It is also proper to have a tag placed or tied to each and every one of the pipes, to identify the kind of ale that is used. Just as soon as the pipes are removed from the coupling, a mistake is liable to be made in changing the pipes. There must be sufficient accommodation in the ale department for shelves, etc., in order to keep tools, such as a mallet, a monkey-wrench, a gimlet, candle and candle dish with the gas fixtures; and a rather warm temperature throughout the year. The pipes must also be cleaned out from time to time, when necessary, and if it is found difficult to have the ales settle, it is advisable to bore a hole with a small-sized gimlet in order to vent the ale, which after this will settle much quicker. A small plug should be placed in the hole, not tighter than to allow the entrance of air, which helps to settle the ale.

There should then be a department for the imported goods, gins, rums, brandies and wines. All the imported liquors in casks should be placed on a skid where the temperature is of medium warmth. If there is room enough, have the shelves placed so they will not be too near the wall, as in the winter time the brick wall of the cellar is liable to be very cold, and the bottled wine would naturally be seriously damaged. All the bottles, as well as other case goods placed on your shelves, must be separated from one another and each have their special department, such as claret, each brand separate on its shelf, and the same with Rhine and Moselle. A plain tag, with name and brand, should be tacked on the separate shelves to prevent any delay in obtaining the bottle desired. In the department of wines, it is often necessary to have a little gas stove that, in case of extreme cold weather, may be lighted to secure the proper temperature, when by neglect or absence of means to heat the place the wines could be spoiled. When a wine is once frozen or chilled it can never be restored to its former condition. This department must have a door that can be closed and locked the same as the ale department.

Then there should be a department for domestic goods, such as American whiskies and case goods. In this department you must also have skids upon which to place your bulk goods, such as whiskey barrels. Above them, if it is convenient, put up a number of shelves, which, as in the other departments, will have arranged upon them each brand in its special separate location. In one of the departments most convenient to you place a table for the purpose of using it in bottling, corking, labelling and wrapping up the goods. Also have sufficient accessories, such as gallon, quart, pint and half-pint measures, mallet, bung starter and the necessary tools all in a tool box, if possible. Have rubber hose for drawing liquors, hammer, hatchet and cold chisel for opening cases; screws and nails of different sizes, for which use will always be found. Additionally, a writing desk and stock or cellar books are needed. Most important of all is a good man, with good habits, in charge of the cellar. I prefer a man who has been brought up to take his daily beverage in moderation and knows how to control himself. A strict temperance man, holding the same position, does not make, as a rule, a very good cellarman or butler, for the reason that he is not acquainted with the different brands of liquors, and, if at any time he "falls from grace," he would probably mix and destroy considerable quantities of goods. If there is one or more cellarmen, the chief one must have entire charge of both cellar and books, and be responsible for the entire stock; because every article removed from the cellar must be noted in gallons and bottles, with prices attached, virtually making a daily inventory of the stock. The same form of bookkeeping must be done and charged behind the bar where the goods are received, so that both accounts will agree or tally in number and price. It is furthermore important that the one who has charge of the cellar should see that he has a sufficient number of quart, pint and half-pint bottles on hand, the proper corks for the different sizes of bottles, flasks, all the various styles of labels required, paper boxes, wrappers, sealing wax and the necessary utensils for bottling goods, with a correct price list or schedule of prices of the different goods, including discount percentage, etc., and the addresses of all wine and liquor dealers with whom he may have business. The cellar should be so built and arranged that it will be easy to ventilate at all seasons; the ceiling in good condition so that no dirt or dust can gather, and be painted or kalsomined in light color. Have also the entire woodwork in all the departments painted, white color being my preference. The iron work, hinges, locks, hasps, etc., should be of a different shade, a black or dark brown, a pretty contrast, and indicating their location. What is absolutely necessary, is a solid, substantial, dry floor, if possible, cemented. If the cellar is built under your own supervision, see that the waste pipes are properly connected with the sewer, a drainer placed over the waste pipe so that, when necessary to clean the floor, it will be convenient to wash it and let the melted ice-water be swept away. When cleaning off the cellar floor, it is wise to dry it with sawdust, to absorb the moisture and then sweep that away, that not a particle of wet or dirt may remain. The names of all the departments should be painted on the door of each one as a guide, and there should also be a general notice painted or printed that no rubbish is to be thrown on the floor, with a caution against spitting except in a cuspidor.

A man who runs a public place should, next to the devotion he gives his family, feel the greatest pride in the arrangement and beautifying of his cellar.

Then he can gladly, at any time, take the public, his friends—ladies and gentlemen—on a tour of inspection of it.

There should be also a department with shelves for empty bottles and wherever placed (sometimes they have been taken outside and then returned), should be thoroughly cleaned with hot water and soda. The drops spilled from the otherwise empty bottles will soon produce a very sour smell if not quickly washed away.

Empty bottles should be kept separate, according to their special brand, the champagne in one place, the claret in another, etc.

A barrel for waste matter and rubbish should be conveniently placed in some part of the cellar. The main door should have a patent bell attached to it, to notify the cellar people that some one is entering. Having all that has been mentioned in a proper style for inspection, you will be gratified to display to visitors the excellence of your management. I am sorry to state, however, that some persons have only regarded the cellar as a dumping ground for all odds and ends, and that is where they have made a grievous mistake. It is to be remembered that stock should be taken about once a month, to ascertain the amount of wines, liquors, etc., on hand.

40. HOW TO CLEAN BRASS AND OTHER METALS.

Most people take pride in having brass and other metal-work look as inviting as possible. This feature may be overdone, however, and altogether too much time expended in polishing the metals. If there is too much metal work, it will destroy the effect of the handsome cabinet and woodwork of the establishment, and also require the services of an additional porter or extra man, adding unnecessarily to the ordinary expenses.

Naturally, brass or metal work, if allowed to become tarnished, looks much worse than if there was none in the place. Properly, in fine condition, it adds to the appearance of bar and room. It is well for any one in opening a place to take into consideration how much metal work, proportionately, they will need, and what amount of expense they are willing to allow for the help to take charge of it. By taking good ordinary care of ale and liquor measures, beer drips and other metal articles, you will find that not half the work, some people imagine, is necessary to keep them bright and shining. All you have to do is to attend to them daily, when they will be as much of an ornament as the chandeliers.

41. KEEPING OF GLASSWARE.

The bartender's particular attention must be given to keeping the glassware in a clean, bright condition. The glasses he hands out to customers for the purpose of allowing them to help themselves, as well as the glasses he uses for mixing drinks, should be without a speck on them. After the glasses are used, they should be washed as soon as possible, left on the bench for a little while to thoroughly drain (those back of the bar being placed at their proper station) and then polished only with a clean linen glass-towel. In a place where there is a hotel or restaurant attached and a large amount of glassware is required, it is proper to have a fine closet made to contain the different kinds of glassware in the proper place, convenient for the waiter and for those who have the handling and are in charge of that department. The glassware should be clean and kept in proper condition by the waiters and not brought back to the bar, as the bartenders are, as a rule, very busy and cannot attend to this duty, being also more liable to break glasses during a rush of business on account of the insufficiency of room. In placing the glassware in the closet, it is understood that all the different grades should be arranged separately, Rhine, champagne, claret, port, etc., each in its special place, for if carerelessly mixed together, there will be great trouble in separating them.

Whoever breaks a glass in the dining-room should report the fact to the head waiter (captain) or assistant head waiter. In a well-regulated bar or café, every bartender should have his own "glass-book," inscribed with his own name, these books to be kept in charge of the cashier behind the bar, so that whenever a glass is broken, accidentally or purposely, by "fooling," it should be reported to the cashier who enters in that special man's book the kind of glass broken. This is not done for the purpose of annoying the bartender, or even with the intention, necessarily, of making him pay for its value, but for the purpose of keeping a proper account of the glassware on hand, and as a reminder to the bartender to be careful. If there is not such a system or control—for it is often the case that both waiters and bartenders become so careless that they would as soon break glasses by the dozen as not—the business is liable to be seriously impaired. With a large concern, where it is understood between employer and employee that all the glass broken must be paid for by them, allowing, naturally, a medium percentage for what can not be helped—that is, the purposely careless bartender or waiter should be obliged to pay for his excessive breakage of glassware—then, there cannot be any feeling of injustice on the part of the em-

PLATE No. 8.

CHAMPAGNE COBBLER.   MINT JULEP.

Copyrighted, 1888.

ployee. Where the employer does sufficient business and can afford to be liberal, he should not think of charging for any amount of moderate breakage. This deducting from the wages may appear unjust to bartenders and waiters, but the best of them are hoping, some day, to become proprietors, and when they are, they will recognize the necessity of this arrangement, for where there is no system in a business enterprise, there will not be success.

42. HOW TO HANDLE ICE.

First of all, it must be understood, before receiving your ice, to have the proper weight taken and, if possible, have your own scales. After receiving and having the weight of the amount of ice you desire, see that it is perfectly clean and washed off before placing it in your ice-box or ice-house.

Of late years, artificial ice has taken to some extent—largely, in the Southern part of the United States—the place of the natural product, which I consider a very beneficial change, for the reason that the artificial cake comes in the same regular size, therefore, easier to pack and place away, more convenient and more wholesome, as it does not contain any impurities. Again, it does not produce as much slime as the natural ice and, therefore, when used behind the bar for mixing drinks, as well as in the restaurant for drinking water, it is preferable, and there is no difficulty in keeping it clear.

Whoever is using artificial ice and is desirous of having a very cold temperature as soon as possible, should not have the cakes of ice placed close together, but leave a small space between them. The air circulating between the cakes helps to cool the ice-box much quicker than if they were packed closely together.

It is also wise not to have the ice-box run down low too often, or too much, for it will take all the longer to get the required temperature you desire for the stock.

It is absolutely necessary to attend to the different ice-boxes every day, and ascertain exactly what amount they require, especially during the summer season. I greatly prefer the artificial ice on account of its cleanliness, handiness and economical price.

In using artificial ice, by dealing with a first-class firm, you will never be disappointed in securing your goods at the proper time and in the quantity desired.

43. THE PURCHASE OF AN OLD PLACE.

In buying out an old business place it is very advisable to be especially careful in the undertaking. First of all, you must consider the locality, then the price asked, whether the place is mortgaged or not, the amount of the mortgage, if mortgaged, and whether to a brewer, liquor dealer, or other individual, the length of time till the mortgage expires, and how much cash money it requires to buy the place and under what conditions. Then ascertain the rent, how long the lease runs, whether it can be extended, and, if so, under what terms the extension is to be made—whether the rent is to be increased or not, a very important matter. Next, find out the amount of business the place has done, how much stock there is on hand, such as liquors, wines, cigars, etc., the condition of the place in its furnishings, cabinet work and plumbing, and whether it requires much improvement or repairs. Then, what the daily expenses have been and what they are likely to be. In figuring up the daily expenses, such as the rent, wages of bartenders, porters, cashier, etc., meals for help, free lunch, gas, ice, laundry, breakage, taxes, coal, number of drinks help are allowed to have, license, insurance, water tax and all the extras, you will know all the actual expenses without which no place can be run.

Of course, every man must know how much help he requires, bartenders, porters, etc. (and if restaurant is attached, waiters, cooks and stewards), and having formulated a perfectly clear statement of your daily expenses, then compare them with the statement of the cash receipts, and you can the more readily know whether the place is worth the money asked or whether it is best to drop out of the proposed transaction. Furthermore, it is advisable to find out whether there are any judgments against the proprietor, or any possible legal proceedings against him, whether or not the place has a bad name, if there is anything detrimental in the neighborhood and if, after consideration of these different points, you have resolved to purchase, it is then wise to ascertain the quantity and quality of goods. If the proposed buyer is not capable of judging correctly, he should take counsel from some one experienced in the business and who understands the measurement of liquors in bulk. It is to be ascertained whether they have been paid for, whether they are sold or consumed by customers on the premises, or whether, as has been the case, a large per cent. of them is sent to other parties by whom they may be used; and the same with wines, cigars, etc. Then a complete inventory should be made of furniture, crockery, silverware, pictures, curtains, etc. Furthermore, it is advisable that the prospective buyer should inquire for all the bills of all the goods sold on the place, for if the seller claims, for instance, to do a business of $50,000 a year, he must be able to produce about or near fifty per cent. of that amount in bills, and by so doing you may be able to compare and see whether his statements are correct or not. Also make inquiries in the neighborhood to ascertain what kind of business has been done, whether the neighbors are in favor of the place, whether the business has been "boomed" by artificial means or not, and what general reasons there could be for the man selling.

Where there is a business transaction involving quite a sum of money, it will frequently require more than your own knowledge and ability, and it is best to engage expert bookkeepers or accountants to examine the cash, stock and other books, bills, receipts, etc., and have every item connected with the business, relating to expenditures and to money received, carefully scanned. At the same time, it is wise not to depend entirely on the statements and judgment of the accountants, for they are liable to make a mistake; but with their assistance and your own judgment, you can find out whether there is any trickery or not in the proposed transaction. Some of the accountants may understand all about bookkeeping but know very little about our business,—as the two forms do not harmonize,—and are therefore liable to make serious errors.

It is necessary to find out by the landlord or from the party selling who pays for all the repairs and in what condition the building is with its floors, windows and walls; and, if it is to be repaired at your expense, how much money it will take to put the place in proper shape. After due deliberation of all the before-mentioned features, and if you have a good opinion of the chances for success, it is advisable, as far as any one can discern, for you to make the investment. It is additionally advisable, if the buyer is not capable of understanding fully the terms of the purchase, the condition of the lease, etc., that he should engage the services of a capable lawyer. Get the good will of the landlord, try to have the lease extended and, in it, have expressly stipulated the amount of rent to be paid.

It is of great importance to find out how many men are to be employed and what wages they are to receive. It has been the case that where a man has paid extraordinary high wages in former years, when prices were higher for goods sold than at present, his successor, in trying the same experiment, has involved himself fatally. Pay as high as you can, a good man is always worth good wages, but do not attempt to give fancy salaries or to increase the wages from year to year, except in exceptional cases.

Finally, it should be stipulated in the bill of sale that the seller should not open another place, similar to yours, within a certain length of time and, then, not within a specified vicinity (five or ten blocks from you, as the understanding may be); for it has often happened that the party who sold has, at once, re-opened another establisment in a near locality, and with all his old help has taken away the trade from the party who has just purchased his old place. This, of course, is a highly dishonorable act, but it has been done many times.

In order to avoid the necessity of reading this entire article, we have itemized the principal points for the consideration of the buyer.

Study the locality, the price asked, see whether it is mortgaged or not, and to whom.

Ascertain the amount of rent, the conditions of the lease and whether the lease can be extended.

Find out the amount of business, how much stock there is on hand, and have inventory taken.

Get complete daily expenses and cash receipts.

Have proof that a certain amount of liquor has actually been consumed on the premises.

Secure proof of the amount of sales.
Employ accountants to inspect the books.
If necessary, engage the services of a legal adviser.
See that the building is in good condition—if necessary to be repaired, find out who pays for repairs.
Be sure that the conditions of the lease are plain.
Study the neighborhood, the people and get acquainted with them.
Stipulate in the bill of sale that the seller shall not open another similar place near you.

44. THE OPENING OF MINERAL WATERS.

It is my desire to make a few remarks regarding the opening of mineral waters. A great many accidents have already occurred whereby people have lost their eyesight or fingers, or received other physical injuries. Therefore, it is wise that every bartender or waiter, and, indeed, every member of a private family should not only try to avoid these accidents, but should also know the proper method to pursue in the opening of apollinaris, soda and other mineral waters.

Bottles containing these should be kept cold and in proper condition, and then they are not as liable to explode as those kept in a warm temperature. But if any one is compelled to open a bottle that is warm, the corkscrew should be inserted carefully in the cork, and then a large-sized napkin or towel wrapped over the top and neck of the bottle so that, if an explosion occurs while the attempt is being made to draw the cork, the cloth will catch the flying pieces of glass and thus prevent any serious injury or mishap.

45. HOW DRINKS SHOULD BE SERVED AT TABLES.

When a bartender receives an order for drinks to be served at tables, he should send the bottles and ice-water along with the glasses on a tray, that the parties may be able to help themselves. If there is a cheque system, the cheque should be sent along at the same time; if not, it is the bartender's duty to mark down the amount at once, in order to avoid confusion or a possible misunderstanding afterward. Even if there is a cheque system, it is advisable for the barkeeper to put the amount of the cheque also on a slate or piece of paper, especially if he does not know the character of his customers. In any restaurant, saloon or hotel where the bartenders have nothing to do with serving customers at a table, and the drinks are called by waiters, it is proper to have small fancy cut (one drink) decanters filled, and sent in by the waiters. This avoids a display of the liquor bottles on the tables, prevents any possibility of liquor being taken by the waiter and has a more becoming appearance. If the customer insists upon seeing the original whiskey or liquor bottle, of course, it is to be taken to him.

46. HOW CLARET WINES SHOULD BE HANDLED.

Claret wines, which must be handled with great care, should be kept in a temperature of 60 to 70 degrees and in a horizontal position. In serving them, especially while drawing the cork, shaking the bottle should be avoided, or the sediment, which all clarets deposit, will be mixed with the wine, causing it to look murky. All the best class of wines should be handled very particularly, and placed first in a wine basket, in a horizontal position. When drawing the cork, the bottle must not be taken out of this basket, but the cork drawn gently, while the bottle remains in its steady position. If too cold, the bartender may have to place the bottle in lukewarm water, or steam the glasses, to give the wine the desired temperature which always improves its flavor.

All the claret wines should be placed on shelves where the temperature is nearly even all the year round. It is advisable for the proprietor to have as large a stock of clarets on hand as possible, providing he has the demand for them, as this brand of wine requires considerable time to rest and recuperate—after being jostled about—from what is known as "wine-sickness." In laying in the stock of clarets, including fancy brands, it is beneficial to take the bottles out of the cases, and remove the wrapping paper before placing the wines in the proper condition on your shelves. Never think of taking down your bottles and dusting them. This only gives the wine another shaking up, requiring days to properly settle, and, again, the dust on the bottles is a proof of its age and condition. It is also of importance, in serving claret wines, to have the proper claret glasses and not a Rhine wine or other kind of goblet or tumbler. The more delicate and handsome your glassware, the more palatable will the wine seem to your customers. People, who drink high-priced liquors, always appreciate glasses of costly make and fine texture. In places where there is a large sale of clarets and the stock of wines is not to be placed in the fit temperature, it is wise to have a closet built and placed—near a radiator, for instance—where the temperature is sufficiently high, in order to keep the wines in proper condition. The closet should be sufficiently large to suit the business requirements, and in it could be placed the stock that would be used in the trade of several days. As it is replenished, day by day, the new bottles can be placed in the rear to allow time for settling. It should be every man's pride to not only keep the best of wines, but, also, to keep them in the best of condition.

47. TREATMENT OF MINERAL WATERS.

It is absolutely necessary to keep mineral waters in a cool place, so that they will be sufficiently cold without the use of ice when being served to customers. Siphons of seltzers or vichy should not be placed directly on ice or in ice water, as there is great danger that they may explode when coming in direct contact with the ice. These waters all contain more or less gas and acid, and should not be subjected to sudden changes of temperature, but, instead, placed in an ice-box, and allowed to cool off, gradually. The proper temperature for mineral waters is from 35 to 50 degrees. This rule applies also to imported goods.

48. IN REFERENCE TO FREE LUNCH.

As it is now the general custom to serve more or less free lunch to patrons, it is of the utmost importance to see that everything you furnish is properly served, and is clean and fit to eat. It is much wiser and better, when circumstances force you to furnish a free lunch, to give not so much in quantity, but of a good quality. When one can do sufficient business without being obliged to set out the lunch, he is fortunate, as it not only saves expense, but avoids considerable trouble. Cheese and crackers, however, are always understood to be in separate bowls on the counter, as some people can not drink without a mouthful to eat, and this trifling food expenditure is enjoyed by those who would never care to be supplied with a free lunch.

Too much lunch should not be cut up, at once, but a little added from time to time, as soon as part of it has been consumed. Sandwiches should be covered with a glass bowl, or napkin, which keeps them fresh and makes them look inviting. When the proprietor is really compelled by business demands to give a large amount of free lunch, he should have an extra man employed for this purpose, who is generally called a regular lunchman. A man of that kind has more experience in cutting and carving, can utilize every bit of the different foods without leaving a remnant to be thrown away. Furthermore, he can overlook the entire lunch-counter, keep it in proper condition, and also have an eye on some customers who are not as particular as they ought to be, and see that the patrons use a fork and not their fingers in digging out or helping themselves to the eatables. If necessary, the lunchman should caution the customer against forgetting the use of the fork, but, of course, he must do it in a gentlemanly manner, or, otherwise, he would offend those who have simply forgotten. There are frequently "roughs" both before and behind the bar. When there is a lunchman stationed behind the counter, it is of great importance for him to be clean and tidy, as well as to handle the lunch with his fingers as little as possible. He should see that all plates and crockery ware are clean, and the crumbs brushed off.

Small, clean napkins are preferable to towels hanging down from the counter. The towel has gone out of use, because common decency does not admit of a variety of men using the same cloth, in wiping their mouths and fingers, brushing their mustaches, and otherwise performing a half-toilet.

It is really a blessing where the proprietor can avoid giving the free lunch. The advantages of a place, where it is not offered to the public, can not be overestimated, for there is then a better class of customers, and the set, who are only in search of a "free meal," do not trouble the establishment with their presence. If obliged to have the free "set-out," the proprietor should suit the style of lunch to the patrons, whether they are Germans, Americans, or Irish, and while the first-named may be pleased with "sauer-kraut" and bologna, it is probable the other classes will not care for that special menu.

The place where the lunch is kept should be scrupulously clean, and no remnants of lunch allowed to be strewn on the floor. If this is neglected, it will result in keeping away from your place of business some of your best patrons who will naturally be disgusted at the lack of cleanliness.

49. HOW TO HANDLE ALE AND PORTER IN CASKS.

In laying in your stock of ale and porter, it is best to have a regular department where nothing but ales and porters are placed, in order to avoid any mixing or confusion with the other kind of casks or barrels. Whenever these liquors are drawn through pipes, the ale department—as it is generally called—should be as near the bar as possible, for the shorter the distance of the ale pipes the more benefit the malt liquors will receive; while the longer the distance the more detrimental they are, because they are liable to give the liquor a bad odor and render it stale. It is especially important to see that the pipes are kept in condition, and that the "packing" of the coupling is in perfect order. These conditions are absolutely essential to give satisfaction to the customer by furnishing him with a fresh beverage, and to prevent a loss that might easily occur by leakage.

Again, the proprietor should own his own faucets (brass, etc.), as he is then free from any obligation to the brewers who have made him a gift of faucets, which he would naturally prefer to return if he changes his line of goods. Then, every brewer has a different patented faucet, and the varying use of them is a source of manifold annoyance to the proprietor.

It is also advisable after the close of the winter season to be especially careful in ordering a supply of malt liquors. As I have recommended, sufficient stock should be on hand during the cold weather, but ordinarily it should later be considerably reduced in amount, for the simple reason that lager beer largely takes its place in consumption, and only half or even quarter-barrels should be purchased.

Bass's ale requires from one to six weeks to get perfectly clear and fit to draw; stock or old ale some weeks, while new ale requires less time. All malt liquors should be tapped as soon as placed on the skids.

50. CORDIALS, BITTERS AND SYRUPS.

Cordials, bitters, and syrups should not be placed on ice, but be kept in a moderate temperature. Those cordials that are used frequently for mixing drinks must be placed in small mixing bottles (see illustration, plate No. 2) behind the bar, and proper care taken to prevent insects from entering them and thus spoiling the contents. In using these mixing bottles, it is advisable to keep one finger on the stopper or

— 139 —

squirt, to prevent it from dropping into the mixing tumbler and thereby waste the material.

In the evening, when business closes, it is advisable to place a small, pointed, wooden plug into the squirt, especially in warm weather, to shut off the possible entrance of flies, ants, and other insects at night. Where there is a use of other cordials, such as are used for pouring in for customers or to be sent to the tables, great care must be taken to have them corked tight, for they contain more or less sweetening substance which attracts insects, flies, etc., necessarily a great nuisance in summer.

51. HOW ALE AND PORTER SHOULD BE DRAWN.

The proper way of drawing ale or porter is directly from the cask or, as it is called, "from the wood." If the necessary room and convenience is available, the customer prefers this to any other method. If drawn through pipes, it is necessary to see that they are made from the best material, such as English block tin, and constantly kept clean, and that the portion remaining in the pipes over night is not used. Otherwise the customer will not be able to obtain a fresh, clear glass of malt liquor. Bottled ales should be stored in a horizontal position, but in a business, where there is a large demand for this beverage, you should also put a large number of bottles in an upright position on your shelves in the ale department, before placing them in the ice-box or refrigerator, as it is necessary with some brands to do this, in order to have them in proper condition. In pouring into glasses, care should be taken not to shake the bottles. In cold weather, it is not necessary to use ice with ale or porter, drawn behind the bar, but if the weather is warm, the temperature may be regulated by allowing ice-water to drop on the pipes constantly. If pouring out Bass's or Scotch ale for one customer, a glass should be selected large enough to hold all that the bottle contains, as otherwise the portion poured out last will not look as clear as it should. If two or three glasses are to be filled, the bartender may take them in his left hand, and carefully pour in the ale by gently tilting the bottle. The liquor will then look perfectly clear and bright, and give entire satisfaction to the customers.

52. DECORATING DRINKS WITH FRUIT.

It is customary to ornament mixed drinks with different kinds of fruit. When drinks are strained, after being mixed, the fruit is placed in the glass, into which the drink is strained; but when straining is not necessary, the fruit is placed on top of the drink, in a tasteful manner. The fruit should be handled with a handsome fruit fork, and not with the fingers, though, in case of a rush, the bartender must do the best he can. It is to be understood that all fruit must be kept very cool and placed where it is not likely to be bothered with flies or other insects. It is to be remarked, also, that where fruit is served with the drink, the bartender should furnish a small bar-spoon to the customer, to enable him to help himself to the fruit in the glass, if he so desires.

53. HOW TO HANDLE FRUITS, EGGS AND MILK.

Eggs, milk, and fruit must always be kept in a cool, well-cleaned place, or in an ice-box, to preserve them fresh and pure. Fruit cut in slices, left over from the day previous, should not be used, as it will taste stale

PLATE No. 9.

FANCY BRANDY SMASH.

Copyrighted, 1883.

and, naturally, spoil a mixed drink. The bartender should be careful to have his milk cans clean, and never pour fresh milk upon that left over night, as it will simply cause both to be sour. Metal pitchers and cans should not be used, but, instead, such of glass or chinaware, and they should not be too large, because, in case the customer desires to help himself, they should be of a convenient size, in order that he may do so readily, without inconvenience. Cans should always be kept tightly closed.

In using eggs for mixed drinks, take a separate glass, into which to put the egg, and you can, therefore, be sure it is fresh before attempting to mix it with the drink. Otherwise, there is always a possibility of spoiling the whole decoction.

54. COVERING BAR FIXTURES WITH GAUZE IN THE SUMMER.

It has been customary, for many years past, to cover the back bar, gas fixtures, chandeliers, pictures, statuary, all decorative articles and furnishings, and fancy fixtures with gauze or some similar form of covering, to keep flies, etc., from soiling them. But I consider this method, though it may be prettily and tastefully arranged, entirely useless, for the reason that experience proves it to be wholly unnecessary. If the place is properly kept and well-ventilated, there is no necessity, whatever, for any covering or draping. In all places, where malt liquor is sold, it is, more or less, spilled and spattered over the floor and counter (and tables, where there are any), and all this tends to cause flies and insects to congregate; but, if the room is kept —as it ought to be—clean and dry, with a perfectly sweet odor, the flies will not become a nuisance. This also applies to the cleanliness of the toilet and everything connected with the place. If it is made a practice to keep in proper order the chandeliers, cabinet, etc., with daily attention, following a set rule, there is very little cleaning to do, and by the additional use of two or more electric fans, which, naturally, keep the room clear of flying pests, you will be able to preserve your entire furnishings in good condition. But with the fixtures covered, you are liable to have the cabinet work injured by nails and tacks of different sizes, in addition to the extra expense.

In case any one prefers to have the covering, it must necessarily be done in a neat, tasteful manner, but it requires very careful adjustment, especially about the gas fixtures, that they may not be liable to be a source of danger and set fire to the gauze. Select elegant, fashionable goods, in quiet colors, and do not have your room look like a circus tent with flashy stripes.

55. CIGARS SOLD AT THE BAR AND ELSEWHERE.

When the proprietor handles or runs his own cigar-stands, it is the bartender's duty to see that they are kept in a proper and elegant condition. Nothing should be ordered but the best brands, imported as well as domestic. Whenever there is a good cigar sold, in a public place, it is very easy to sell more, as your customers will speak of it, and thus help to advertise your goods.

Men in our business should not try to secure too large a profit from cigars, because, as a rule, a good cigar is a good advertisement, and trade will come to you freely, if you are satisfied with a fair profit. No one should sell without a profit, but a medium percentage of gain should be sufficient to satisfy the proprietor, for the simple reason that by retaining a good customer for his cigars, he also, probably, has gained one for his bar, or his restaurant, or both.

It is not wise to buy too large a quantity of cigars, at one time, for different reasons. In the first place, you can secure goods, on very short notice, in a fresh condition. When you have too much stock on hand, the cigars are liable to become dry, and lose their flavor.

With the cigars under the eyes or management of the bartender, he must see that the entire stock in the case is kept properly in the summer as well as in the winter. In warm weather, there is less trouble in keeping cigars, because the natural heat produces a moisture in the case, and this keeps the goods in about the condition required by customers. During the winter, however, when the rooms are artificially heated, the cigars are apt to become dry very readily; and this dryness is very detrimental to the entire stock, causing the wrappers to break easily by constant handling, when, of course, the customers will be dissatisfied with them. Therefore, every cigar-case or cigar-stand should be made with all the latest improvements, including air-tight compartments or closets. Underneath the closet, as well as underneath the cigar-case, little drawers should be made, containing little metal boxes of the same width as that of the closet. In these cases a metal pan should be placed, filled partly with water, and with a very fine perforated cover to the pans to allow the evaporation of the water from the pan into the cigar-case or closets, in order to keep the cigars in a properly moist condition. It is not only correct to handle the best of cigars, but, also, to handle the latest brands, for the fashion changes in cigars, as in almost everything else, and, if not careful, the proprietor will be left with old, unsalable stock on hand.

In a place where there is a large sale of imported goods, it is advisable to have an extra closet built which should be lined with zinc, and made perfectly air-tight, so that the goods will not become dry. Where there is a very small, improperly arranged cigar-case, a large-sized sponge, saturated with water, will be sufficient to give proper moisture to the cigars. But, as a rule, in large establishments the cigar-stands are entirely separated from the café or bar, and are generally rented out to a second party, this method being usually very satisfactory and saving much trouble.

When the proprietor expects to sell a large amount of cigars, it requires the sole attention of one man to keep the case in order, wait on customers, study their desires and wants, and, by striving to please, recommending certain brands, etc., a large income can be derived daily from the sale of cigars, by an earnest, energetic, polite salesman.

56. LAST BUT NOT LEAST.

I can not avoid, very well, offering a few more remarks regarding the conduct and appearance of the bartender, although I have touched upon the subject quite frequently in this book. I wish to impress on the mind of each man behind the bar, that he should look and act as neatly as possible. Bartenders should not, as some have done, have a tooth-pick in their mouth, clean their finger-nails while on duty, smoke, spit on the floor, or have other disgusting habits. If it can be avoided, they should not eat their meals behind the bar. There are other places where these things can be done, and where they will not be objectionable features for the patrons of a place. After leaving a toilet-room a bartender should wash his hands, which, at all times, should be as clean and dry as possible. The swaggering air some bartenders have, and by which they think they impress the customers with their importance, should be studiously avoided.

57. COMPLETE LIST OF UTENSILS, Etc. Used in a Bar Room.

In giving the annexed list of utensils, used in a bar room, the author wishes it understood that not all the articles mentioned are absolutely necessary in every bar room, but they are indispensable in those places where the business demands call for them, for instance, in first-class bar rooms.

Cash Registers,
Liquor Measures:
Gallon,
Half-Gallon,
Quart,
Pint,
Half-Pint,
Gill,
Half-Gill,
Liquor Pump,
Mallet,
Filtering Bag or Paper,
Beer and Ale Faucets,
Brace and Bit,
Liquor Gauge,
Gimlet,
Beer and Ale Measures,
Bung Starter,
Rubber Hose for drawing Liquor,
Liquor Thieves,
Thermometer,
Funnels,
Corkscrews,
Hot Water Kettle,
Bar Pitchers,
Lemon Squeezers,
Beer and Ale Vent,
Ice Pick,
Ice Cooler,
Ice Shaver,
Ice Scoop,
Liquor Gigger,
Shaker,
Long twisted and short Bar Spoons,
Julep and Milk Punch Strainers,
Spice Dish or Castor,
Ale Mugs,
Cork Pullers,
Glass and Scrubbing Brush,
Corks and Stoppers (different sizes),
Cork Press,
Champagne Faucets, for drawing Wine out of Bottles,
Molasses Jugs or Pitchers,
Honey or Syrup Pitchers,
Lemon Knives,
Sugar Spoons,
Sugar Tongues,
Wrapping Paper for Bottled Goods.

Toothpicks,
Twine,
Writing Paper,
Envelopes,
Postal Cards,
Stamps,
Ink,
Mucilage,
Rattan,
Business Cards,
Business Directory,
City Directory,
Newspapers,
Set of Books,
Wash Soap,
Washing Soda,
Demijohns (large and small),
Bar Bottles,
Mixture Bottles,
Quart Flasks,
Pint Flasks,
Half-Pint Flasks,
Segar Bags,
Julep Straws,
Sponge,
Window Brush,
Egg Beaters,
Sugar Pails,
Nutmeg Box,
Nutmeg Grater,
Cracker Bowls,
Sugar Bowls,
Punch or Tom and Jerry Bowls,
Tom and Jerry Cups,
Pepper Boxes,

Fruit Dishes,
Punch Ladles,
Duster and Broom,
Silver Brush,
Segar Cutter,
Mop Handle and Wringer,
Glass Towels,
Rollers,
Bar Towels,
Spittoons,
Fancy Fruit Forks,
Fancy Sugar Plate or Basket,
Liquor Labels,
Pails for Waste,
Match Boxes and Matches
Comb and Brush,
Toilet Paper,
Whiting for cleaning Silverware,
Dust Pan,
Shot for cleaning Bottles,
Step-Ladder,
Waiters or Trays,
Oil for oiling the Fixtures,
Table Salt and Celery Salt Boxes,
Railroad Guide (containing the time-table for information of different roads),
Ruler (for skimming off Beer froth),
Hammer,
Screws and Nails.

58. LIST OF GLASSWARE
Required in a Bar Room or Cafe.

Goblets for Champagne and special glasses for the following drinks:

Burgundy Wine,
Bordeaux Wine,
Champagne Cocktail,
Champagne,
John and Tom Collins,
Julep or Cobbler,
Claret Wine,
Rhine Wine,
Port Wine,
Sherry Wine,
Mineral Water,
Hot Water,
Fancy Glass Pitchers for the different kinds of Cups, as Champagne and Claret Cups, etc.,
Tom and Jerry Mugs,
Finger Bowls (for placing your Bar Spoons and Strainers),
Absinthe Strainer,
Cocktail and Sour,
Whiskey,
Pony Brandy,
Cordial,
Water,
Hot Apple Toddy,
Ale, Porter and Beer,
Pony Beer,
Stanga (shell) Beer Glass,
Stine Mugs,
Ale Mugs,
Fizz Glass,
Glass Jars for Julep Straws.

In buying glassware match them as near as possible, and have them all the same style.

---

59. LIST OF DIFFERENT LIQUORS
That are required in a Bar Room.

Brandy (different brands if required),
Bourbon Whiskey,
Scotch Whiskey,
Old Tom Gin,
St. Croix Rum,
Blackberry Brandy,
Spirits,
Rye Whiskey,
Irish Whiskey,

Holland Gin,
Jamaica Rum,
Apple Jack or Brandy,
Arrack,
Medford Rum,
Antigua,
Meder Swan Gin,
De Kuyper Gin,
Sloe Gin,
Burnett's Old Tom Gin,
Booth's Old Tom Gin,
Geneva Gin,
Creme de Holland Gin,
Fockink's Gin,
Gordon's Gin,
King Charles Gin,
London Cordial Gin,
Mistletoe Gin,
Nicholson's Dry Gin,
Old Holland Gin,
Plymouth Gin,
Posthorn Gin,
Red Lion Gin,
Swan Gin,
Wolfe's Schnapps,
Burk's Irish Whiskey,
Buchanan's Scotch Whiskey,
Dewar's Scotch Whiskey,
Jno. Jameson Whiskey,
Kinahan L. L. Irish Whiskey,
King William Scotch Whiskey,
Robertson & Sons' Plain Scotch Whiskey,
Stewart's Finest Scotch Whiskey,
Ushers' Scotch Whiskey,
Walker's Scotch Whiskey,
Antediluvian Rye Whiskey,
Canadian Club Whiskey,
Carstairs' Rye Whiskey,
Cutter's Whiskey,
Hunter Rye Whiskey,
Maryland Club Rye Whiskey,
Mount Vernon Whiskey,
Old Crow Whiskey,
Old Jordan Whiskey,
James E. Pepper & Co. Whiskey,
Henry Clay Whiskey,
Pickwick Club Whiskey,
Mitchell's Irish Whiskey,
Robertson & Co. Whiskey,
Runnymede Rye Whiskey,
Trimble Whiskey,
Wilson Whiskey,
Ten Year Old Whiskey,
Stability Whiskey,
Tennessee Smash Whiskey,
Royal Cabinet Whiskey,

The above are a few of the most popular brands of liquors now in use.

60. LIST OF PRINCIPAL WINES.

Champagne (Piper Heidsieck & Co.),
Sauterne Wines,
Rhine and Moselle Wines,
Bordeaux Wines,
Catawba Wines,
Spanish Wines,
Port (red and white) Wines,
Claret Wines,
Madeira Wines,
Hungarian (red and white) Wines,
California Wines,
Tokay Wines,
Sherry Wines,
Burgundy Wines,

61. LIST OF PRINCIPAL CORDIALS.

The list below contains the principal kinds used for mixing drinks; if others are required they can be procured.

Absinthe (green and white),
Curaçoa (red and white),
Maraschino Dalmatico,
Creme de Mocca,
Anisette de Martinique,
Eau d'Amour (Liebeswasser),
Vermouth,
Allash Russian Kummel,
Vanille,
Creme d'Ananas,
China-China,
Creme d'Anisette,
Huile de Fleurs d'Oranges
Creme de Peppermint,
Amourette,
Eau de Calame (calmus liqueur),
Creme de Nagau,
Creme de Chocolate,
Angelica,
Eau Celeste (Himmels-Wasser),
Boonekamp of Magbitter,
Creme au lait (Milk Liqueur),
Benedictine,
Chartreuse (green and yellow),
Eau d'Or (Goldwasser),
Parfait d'Amour,
Curaçoa de Marseille,
Kirschwasser,
Anisette,
Danziger Goldwasser,
Bouquet de Dames,
Berlin Gilka,
Eau de Belles Femmes,
Huile d'Angelica,

Eau de Pucelle (Jungfern Wasser),
Maraschino di Zara,
Curaçoa Imperial,
Creme aux Bergamottes,
Creme de Canelle,
Mint Cordial,
Eau d'Argent (Silberwasser),
Creme de Cocoa,
Krambambuli,
Creme de Menthe (Pfefferminz liqueur),
Creme aux Amandes (Mandel Creme),
Liqueur de la Grande Chartreuse (green),
Creme de Noisette à la Rose,
Liqueur de la Grande Chartreuse (yellow),
Liqueur de la Grande Chartreuse (white),
Creme de Noyaux,
Creme de Cacao-Chuao,
Prunelle,
Creme de Pekoe,
Abricotine Liqueur,
Mandarin,

62. LIST OF ALES AND PORTER.

Bass Ale in casks and bottles,
Scotch Ales (Muir & Son),
Scotch Ales (Robert Younkers),
New and Old Ales,
Bottled Beer (domestic and imported),
McMullen's White Label (bottles),
Dog's Head Bass,
Arf and Arf,
Guiness' Extra Stout in casks and bottles (imported),
Stock Ales,
Porter, Lagerbeer,
Bottled Ales and Porter, (domestic and imported),

63. LIST OF THE PRINCIPAL MINERAL WATERS.

Belfast Ginger Ale,
Kissengen Waters,
Congress Waters,
Vichy Waters,
Lemon and Plain Soda Waters,

Sarsaparilla,
Carbonic Acid,
White Rock,
Buffalo Lithia,
Domestic Ginger Ale,
Apollinaris Waters,
Imp. Selters Waters,
Syphon Selters, Vichy and Carbonic,

Hathorn Waters,
Cider,
Acid Syphon,
Poland Water,
Saratoga Vichy,
Hunyadi Water,
Carlsbad Water,
Apenta Water.

64. LIST OF PRINCIPAL SYRUPS.

White Gum Syrup,
Pineapple Syrup,
Strawberry Syrup,
Raspberry Syrup,
Lemon Syrup,

Orange Syrup,
Orchard Syrup,
Orgeat Syrup,
Rock Brandy Syrup.

65. LIST OF PRINCIPAL BITTERS.

Bokers (the genuine only),
Hostetter's Bitters,
Orange Bitters,
Boonecamp Bitters,

Stoughton Bitters,
Sherry Wine Bitters,
East India Bitters.
Angostura,

66. LIST OF THE PRINCIPAL FRUITS Used in a Cafe.

Apples,
Peaches,
Limes,
Grapes,
Blackberries,
Oranges,

Lemons,
Pineapples,
Strawberries,
Preserved Cherries,
Olives.

67. LIST OF PRINCIPAL MIXTURES.

Tansy,
Calamus or Flag Root,
Black Molasses,
Milk,
Jamaica Ginger,
Mint,
Honey,
Wormwood,
Eggs,
Sugar (lumps and pulverized),
Peppermint,
Peper (red and black),
Condensed Milk,
Nutmeg,

Allspice,
Cinnamon,
Salt,
Pepper Sauce,
Bicarbonate of Soda,
Calisaya,
Cloves,
Coffee,
Roast Corn,
Celery Salt,
Beef Extract,
Celery Syrup,
Bromo Lithia,
Bromo Seltser,
Antipareen.

68. SUNDRIES.

Segars,
Cigarettes,

Tobaccos,
Chewing Tobacco.

69. THE PRINCIPAL STOCK OF A RESTAURANT.

Meats,
Beef,
Mutton,
Lamb,
Veal,
Pork,

Vegetables,
Potatoes,
Onions,
Tomatoes,
Cabbage,
Lettuce,

Spinach,
Fish,
Shell Fish,
Oysters,
Clams,
Terrapin,
Green Turtle,
Crabs,
Soft Shell Crabs,
Lobsters,
Turtle,
Shad roe,
Crab Meat,
Groceries of all descriptions, as Allspices, Salts, Pepper, etc.,
Eggs,
Butter,
Poultry,
Coffee,
Bread,
Sausages,
Tongues,
Calf's Brains,
Livers,
Kidneys,
Ice Cream,
Hams,
Corned Beef,
Mushrooms,
Milk,
Tea,
Cream,
Rolls,
Fruit,
Cheese,

Cakes,
Pickles,
Biscuits,
Crackers,
Pies,
Vinegar,
Lemons,
Oranges,
Apples,
Grapes,
Grape Fruit,
Bananas,
Water Cress,
Muffins,
Pig's Feet,
Water Melons,
Musk Melons,
Cantelopes,
Beets,
Strawberries,
Huckleberries,
Blackberries,
Chow Chow,
Pepper Hash,
Olive Oil,
Lard,
Olives,
Radishes,
Capers,
Cherries,
Peaches,
Pears,
Cranberries,
Figs, Dates, etc.,
Cucumbers,
Plums.

70. THE PRINCIPAL STOCK OF A CAFE.

Whiskeys in bulk, as American, Scotch and Irish;
Domestic and imported Beer in casks as well as in bottles;
Champagnes, Piper Heidsieck, etc.;
Rhine Wines;
Moselle Wines;
Claret Wines, etc., such as Sherry and Port Wines;
Mineral Waters, as Apolinaris, Selters, Carbonic, Vichy, Imported German Seltzer, Ginger Ale, Soda, Sarsaparilla, Buffalo Lithia, White Rock, etc.;
Ales and Porters in bulk and bottles;
Cordials of all kinds;
Jamaica Rum, Medford Rum, St. Croix Rum, etc.;
Holland, Old Tom, Sloe Gin, etc.;
Brandies;
Bitters;
Fruits used in dressing drinks, such as Lemons, Limes, Oranges, Pine Apple, Peppermint, etc.;
Milk and Cream;
Cider and Apple Jack;
Cherries in Maraschino, used for dressing cocktails;
Olives, used for dressing cocktails;
Arrack.

PLATE No. 10.

WHISKEY DAISY.

Copyrighted, 1888.

CHAMPAGNE COCKTAIL.

(Use a champagne goblet.)

In mixing all the different cocktails it is proper to fill the mixing tumbler with fine-shaved or broken ice, before putting in any of the ingredients, as it has a much better appearance, but in mixing a champagne cocktail it is the proper way of having two or three lumps of clear crystal ice, place them on the bottom of your glass, and mix as follows:

2 or 3 small lumps of crystal ice;
1 or 2 slices of orange placed on top of ice;
2 or 3 nice strawberries, if in season;
1 fine slice of pine-apple;
1 lump of loaf sugar, placed on top of ice;
2 or 3 dashes of bitters (Boker's genuine only).

In all First-Class Bar Rooms Boker's Genuine Bitters is still in demand as much as ever.

Fill the champagne cocktail glass with wine (Piper-Heidsieck), stir up with a spoon, and twist the oil of a nice piece of lemon peel on top of this, and serve. If it should happen, as it is often the case, that a party of two or three should enter a bar room and call for a champagne cocktail, the proper way would be for a bartender to inquire what kind of wine they desire. Piper-Heidsieck generally being used, a small bottle is sufficient for three cocktails, and also see that the sugar is handled, at all times, with a pair of tongues, and the fruit with a fruit fork; this is strictly to be observed in mixing the above drink (see illustration, plate No. 4).

POUSSE CAFE.
(Use a sherry wine glass.)

In mixing the above drink, which is a favorite drink of the French, and also has become a favorite in this country, great care must be taken. As there are several liquors required in the preparation of this drink, it should be made in a manner that the portions will be perfectly separated from each other; therefore I would suggest, that a sherry-wine glass should be used for pouring in these different cordials, instead of a teaspoon or the original bottles, as it has a better appearance and takes less time. Mix as follows:

$1/6$ glass of parfait d'amour or raspberry syrup;
$1/6$ glass of maraschino;
$1/6$ glass of vanilla (green);
$1/6$ glass of curaçao (red);
$1/6$ glass of chartreuse (yellow);
$1/6$ glass of cognac or brandy (Martell).

The above ingredients will fill the glass (see illustration, plate No. 6).

I would advise every bartender, having calls for these drinks often, to place his original bottles containing the different cordials, which are being used in the drink, separated in one place, so as to have them follow in rotation, as above mentioned: this will avoid mixing up the bottles and save much trouble. I also have to mention another item of great importance, and that is, that the cordials used in the above drink differ in weight; for instance, you will find the French curaçao to weigh more than the Holland curaçao, and so it is different in all cordials; therefore it is wise for a bartender to find out the different weights, and then place them in rotation, in order to avoid mixing up, as you cannot depend entirely on the illustration in mixing the drink called "pousse café." (This drink is generally taken after meals.)

(See illustration, plate No. 6.)

MINT JULEP

(Use a large fancy bar glass.)

1 small table-spoonful of sugar;
½ wine-glass of water or selters;
3 or 4 sprigs of fresh mint; dissolve with sugar and water, until the flavor of the mint is well extracted; then take out the mint, and add
1½ wine-glass of brandy (Martell).

Fill the glass with fine-shaved ice; stir well, then take some sprigs of mint, and insert them in the ice with stem downward, so that the leaves will be on surface in the shape of a bouquet; ornament with berries, pine-apple, and orange on top in a tasty manner; dash with a little Jamaica rum, and sprinkle with a little sugar on top; serve with a straw.

This drink is known not only in this country, but in all parts of the world, by name and reputation (see illustration, plate No. 8).

CURACOA PUNCH.

(Use a large bar glass.)

½ table-spoonful of sugar;
2 or 3 dashes of lemon juice;
½ wine-glass of water or selters, dissolve well with a spoon, and fill up the glass with fine-shaved ice;
½ wine-glass of brandy (Martell);
1 wine-glass of curaçao (red);
½ pony-glass of Jamaica rum; stir up well with a spoon, ornament with grapes, pine-apple, oranges, berries, and cherries (if in season), and serve with a straw.

The above drink, if mixed correctly, is very delicious (see illustration, plate No. 12).

MORNING GLORY FIZZ.
(Use a large bar glass.)

In all first-class bar rooms it is proper to have the whites of eggs separated into an empty bottle, provided you have a demand for such a drink, and keep them continually on ice, as, by doing so, considerable time will be saved; mix as follows:
1 fresh egg (the white only);
¾ table-spoonful of sugar;
1 or 2 dashes of lemon juice;
2 or 3 dashes of lime juice;
3 or 4 dashes of absinthe, dissolve well with a little water or selters;
¾ glass filled with fine-shaved ice;
1 wine-glass of Scotch whiskey.

Shake up well with a shaker; strain it into a good-sized bar glass; fill up the balance with syphon selters or vichy water, and serve.

The above drink must be drank as soon as prepared, so as not to lose the effect and flavor. The author respectfully recommends the above drink as an excellent one for a morning beverage, which will give a good appetite and quiet the nerves (see illustration, plate No. 7).

MANHATTAN COCKTAIL.
(Use a large bar glass.)

Fill the glass up with ice;
1 or 2 dashes of gum syrup, very carefully;
1 or 2 dashes of bitters (orange bitters);
1 dash of curaçao or absinthe, if required;
½ wine-glass of whiskey;
½ wine-glass of vermouth;

Stir up well; strain into a fancy cocktail glass; squeeze a piece of lemon peel on top, and serve; leave it for the customer to decide, whether to use absinthe or not. This drink is very popular at the present day. It is the bartender's duty to ask the customer, whether he desires his drink dry or sweet.

BRANDY CRUSTA.
(Use a large bar glass.)

Take a nice, clean lemon of the same size as your wine-glass, cut off both ends of it, and peel it in the same way as you would peel an apple; put the lemon peel in the wine-glass, so that it will line the entire inside of the glass, then dip the edge of the glass and the lemon peel in pulverized sugar; take your mixing glass and mix as follows:

3 or 4 dashes of orchard syrup;
1 or 2 dashes of bitters (Boker's genuine only);
4 or 5 drops of lemon juice;
2 dashes of maraschino;
$\frac{3}{4}$ of the glass filled with fine ice;
1 wine-glass of brandy (Martell).

Stir up well with a spoon, strain it into the glass, dress with a little fruit, and serve (see illustration, plate No. 5).

ABSINTHE COCKTAIL.
(Use a large bar glass.)

Fill up with ice;
3 or 4 dashes of gum syrup;
1 dash of bitters (Boker's genuine only);
1 dash anisette;
$\frac{1}{4}$ wine-glass of water or imported selters;
$\frac{3}{4}$ wine-glass of absinthe.

Shake well until almost frozen or frapped; strain it into a fancy cocktail glass squeeze a lemon peel on top, and serve.

This drink is liked by the French and by the Americans; it is an elegant beverage and a splendid appetizer; but see that you always have the genuine absinthe only for mixing this drink.

CHAMPAGNE JULEP.
(Use a fancy julep glass.)

Take the sugar tongues, and place 1 medium-sized lump of loaf sugar into the glass, add 1 sprig of fresh mint, then pour your champagne (Piper-Heidsieck) into the glass very slowly, and, while doing so, keep on stirring gently all the time; place some slices of oranges, pine-apples, and a few strawberries; ornament the top in a very tasty manner; then serve.

The above drink does not require to be stirred up as much as other juleps, else the champagne will lose its flavor and natural taste, and foam too much (see illustration, plate No. 14).

BRANDY SHAMPARELLE.
(Use a sherry wine glass.)

¼ wine glass of curacoa (red);
¼ wine glass of chartreuse (yellow);
¼ wine glass of anisette;
¼ wine glass of Kirschwasser or brandy (Martell), whichever the customer desires.

Attention must be paid to prevent the different liquors from running into each other, to have them perfectly separated and distinct. Use a sherry glass for pouring in your different cordials instead of a teaspoon, for the reason that it looks better and accomplishes the work much quicker (see illustration, plate No. 6).

MARTINI COCKTAIL.
(Use a large bar glass.)

Fill the glass up with ice;
2 or 3 dashes of gum syrup (be careful in not using too much);
2 or 3 dashes of bitters (Boker's genuine only);
1 dash of curaçao or absinthe, if required;
½ wine-glass of old Tom gin;
½ wine-glass of vermouth.
Stir up well with a spoon; strain it into a fancy cocktail glass; put in a cherry or a medium-sized olive, if required; and squeeze a piece of lemon peel on top, and serve (see illustration, plate No. 13).

POUSSE L'AMOUR.
(Use a sherry wine glass.)

This delicious French drink is somewhat similar to the "pousse café," and also has to be carefully made; mix as follows:
¼ sherry-glass of maraschino; **drop in**
1 yolk of a fresh egg;
¼ glass of vanilla (green);
¼ glass of cognac (Martell).
Proper attention must be paid that the yolk of the egg is fresh and cold, and that it does not run into the liquor, in order to have it in its natural form (see illustration, plate No. 6).

SILVER FIZZ.
(Use a large bar glass.)

½ table-spoonful of sugar;
2 or 3 dashes of lemon juice
1 wine-glass of Old Tom gin, dissolved well, with a squirt of vichy;

1 egg (the white only);
¾ glass filled with shaved ice.

Shake up well with a shaker; strain it into a good-sized fizz-glass; fill up the glass with syphon, vichy, or selters; mix well, and serve.

This drink is a delicious one, and must be drank as soon as prepared, as it loses its strength and flavor.

MISSISSIPPI PUNCH.
(Use a large bar glass.)

1 small table-spoonful of sugar;
½ wine-glass of vichy or selters;
2 dashes of lemon juice, dissolved well;
½ wine-glass of Jamaica rum;
½ wine-glass of Bourbon whiskey;
¾ wine-glass of brandy (Martell).

Fill the glass with shaved ice; shake or stir the ingredients well; ornament in a tasty manner with fruit in season, and serve with a straw (see illustration, plate No. 12).

ROMAN PUNCH.
(Use a large bar glass.)

½ table-spoonful of sugar;
½ pony-glass of raspberry syrup;
2 or 3 dashes of lemon or lime juice, dissolved with a little vichy or selters;
¼ pony-glass of curaçao;
½ wine-glass of brandy (Martell);
½ pony-glass of Jamaica rum.

Stir up well with a spoon; ornament the top with grapes, oranges, pine-apple, etc., if in season; and serve with straw.

This is one of the oldest drinks known in Europe as well as in this country (see illustration, plate No. 14).

WHISKEY DAISY.
(Use a large bar glass.)

½ table-spoonful of sugar;
2 or 3 dashes of lemon juice;
1 dash of lime juice;
1 squirt of syphon, vichy, or selters; dissolve with the lemon and lime juice;
¾ of the glass filled with fine-shaved ice;
1 wine-glass of good whiskey;
Fill the glass with shaved ice;
½ pony-glass chartreuse (yellow).

Stir up well with a spoon; then take a fancy glass, have it dressed with fruits in season, and strain the mixture into it, and serve.

This drink is very palatable and will taste good to almost anybody (see illustration, plate No. 10).

CHAMPAGNE COBBLER.
(Use a large bar glass.)

¼ of a table-spoonful of sugar;
¼ wine-glass of syphon selters; dissolve well;
1 or 2 pieces of oranges;
1 or 2 pieces of pine-apple;
Fill the glass with shaved ice;
Fill the balance with champagne (Piper-Heidsieck).

Stir up very gently, so that the foam of the wine does not overflow; ornament the top in a tasty manner, and serve it with a straw.

This drink is generally mixed where they have champagne on draught, by having the champagne faucet screwed into the cork of the bottle (see illustration, plate No. 8).

TOLEDO PUNCH.
(Use a large punch bowl.)

This punch is only prepared for parties, and the author composed it for one of the most prominent establishments in the West, and styled it "Toledo." Mix as follows:

Place 2 pounds of loaf sugar in the bowl;
4 or 5 bottles of plain soda water;
4 lemons (the juice only);
1 glass of French cognac (Martell);
1 small bunch of wintergreen;
4 oranges and 1 pine-apple (cut up), and add the slices into the bowl, and also strawberries and grapes, if in season.

Mix the ingredients well with a spoon or ladle, then add:

6 bottles of champagne (Piper-Heidsieck);
½ bottle of brandy;
2 bottles of French claret;
4 bottles of Rhine wine;
4 quart bottles of imported German seltser water;
and mix up well together into the bowl, and you will have one of the finest punches ever made.

It is to be understood that this punch must be cold, therefore surrounded with ice, in the same way as other punches.

After having well mixed the entire punch, take a large fancy goblet, and fill it with the above mixture; then dress it with oranges, strawberries, pine-apples, etc., if in season.

GOLDEN SLIPPER.
(Use a sherry wine glass.)

½ wine-glass of chartreuse (yellow);
1 yolk of a fresh cold egg;
½ wine-glass of "Danziger Goldwasser."

The above drink is a great favorite of the ladies from Southern America, and must be mixed in a very careful manner, so that the yolk of the egg does not run into the liquor, and keep its form; use a sherry-glass in mixing, instead of a spoon (see illustration, plate No. 13).

EGG NOGG.
(Use a large bar glass.)

1 fresh egg;
$\frac{3}{4}$ table-spoonful of sugar;
$\frac{1}{3}$ glass full of ice;
1 pony-glass St. Croix or Jamaica rum;
1 wine-glassful of brandy (Martell).

Fill the glass with rich milk; shake or stir with a spoon the ingredients well together, and strain into a large bar glass; grate a little nutmeg on top, and serve. It is proper for the bartender to ask the customer what flavor he prefers, whether St. Croix or Jamaica rum. It is wise to be careful, not to put too much ice into your mixing goblet, as by straining you might not be able to fill the glass properly, as it ought to be.

SHERRY COBBLER.
(Use a large bar glass.)

$\frac{1}{2}$ table-spoonful of sugar;
$\frac{1}{2}$ wine-glass of selters water, dissolve with a spoon;
Fill the glass up with fine crystal ice;
Then fill the glass up with sherry wine;

Stir well with spoon, and ornament with grapes, oranges, pine-apples, berries, etc.; serve with a straw.

This drink is without doubt the most popular beverage in the country, with ladies as well as with gentlemen. It is a very refreshing drink for old and young.

FANCY WHISKEY SMASH.
(Use a large bar glass.)

½ table-spoonful of sugar;
½ glass of water, or squirt of selters;
3 or 4 sprigs of mint, dissolve well with a spoon;
Fill the glass full of fine-shaved ice;
1 wine-glass of whiskey.

Stir up well with a spoon; strain it into a fancy sour glass; ornament with fruit, and serve.

This drink requires particular care and attention, so as to have it palatable and look proper.

CHAMPAGNE SOUR.
(Use a fancy glass.)

1 lump of loaf sugar;
1 dash of fresh lemon juice.

Place the saturated sugar into a fancy glass, also a slice of orange and a slice of pine-apple, a few strawberries or grapes (if in season); fill up the glass slowly with champagne (Piper-Heidsieck), and stir up well; then serve it (see illustration, plate No. 5).

KNICKERBOCKER.
(Use a large bar glass.)

2 table-spoonfuls of raspberry syrup;
2 dashes of lemon juice;
1 slice of pine-apple;
1 slice of orange;
1 wine-glassful of St. Croix rum;
½ wine-glass of curaçao.

Then fill the glass with fine-shaved ice; stir or shake well, and dress with fruit in season; serve with a straw.

VANILLA PUNCH,
(Use a large bar glass.)

1 small table-spoonful of sugar;
2 or 3 dashes of lime or lemon juice;
2 or 3 dashes of curaçao, dissolve well with a little water or selters;
Fill up the glass with shaved ice;
½ pony-glass of brandy (Martell);
1½ wine-glass of vanila.

Mix well with a spoon; ornament with fruit in a tasty manner, and serve with a straw.

SHERRY FLIP.
(Use a large bar glass.)

1 fresh egg;
½ table-spoonful of sugar;
½ glassful of shaved ice;
1½ wine-glassful of sherry wine.

Shake it well, until it is thoroughly mixed; strain it into a fancy bar glass; grate a little nutmeg on top, and serve.

This is a very delicious drink, and gives strength to delicate people (see illustration, plate No. 15).

WHISKEY RICKEY.
(Use a medium size fizz glass.)

1 or 2 pieces of ice;
Squeeze the juice of 1 good-sized lime or 2 small ones;
1 wine-glass of rye whiskey.

Fill up the glass with club soda, selters, or vichy; and serve with spoon.

FANCY BRANDY COCKTAIL.
(Use a large bar glass.)

¾ glass filled with shaved ice;
2 or 3 dashes of gum syrup;
1 or 2 dashes of bitters (Boker's genuine only);
1 or 2 dashes of curacoa or absinthe, if required;
1 glass of French brandy (Martell).

Stir well with a spoon; strain into a fancy cocktail glass, and squirt a little champagne into it; also put a cherry in; twist a piece of lemon peel on top, and serve. The champagne will only be added where it is kept on draught.

Mixed as directed, the above will make a very pleasant drink. It is a universal favorite in the western part of this country.

BRANDY PUNCH.
(Use a large bar glass.)

¾ table-spoonful of sugar;
A few drops of pine-apple syrup;
1 or 2 dashes of lemon juice;
1 or 2 dashes of lime juice;
1 squirt of selters, dissolve with a spoon;
Fill up glass with finely shaved ice;
1½ wine-glassfuls of old brandy (Martell).

Stir up well; flavor with a few drops of Jamaica rum, and ornament with grapes, oranges, pine-apple, and berries; then serve with a straw.

WHITE LION.
(Use a large bar glass.)

1 small table-spoonful of sugar;
2 or 3 dashes of lime or lemon juice, dissolve well with a little seltzer;
½ pony-glass of raspberry syrup;

PLATE No. 11.

FANCY BRANDY SOUR.

Copyrighted, 1888.

¼ pony-glass of curaçao;
Fill up glass with shaved ice;
1 wine-glassful of St. Croix rum.
Stir up well with a spoon; ornament with the fruits of the season; serve with a straw.
This drink is known for a great number of years in South America.

BALTIMORE EGG NOGG.
(Use a large bar glass.)

1 yolk of a fresh egg;
¾ table-spoonful of sugar;
Add a little nutmeg and cinnamon, and beat to a cream;
½ pony-glass of brandy (Martell);
3 or 4 lumps of ice;
¼ pony-glass of Jamaica rum;
1 wine-glassful of Madeira wine.
Fill the glass with milk, shake well, strain into a large bar glass, grate a little nutmeg on top, and serve.

ST. CHARLES PUNCH.
(Use a large bar glass.)

1 small table-spoonful of sugar;
2 or 3 dashes of lemon juice, dissolve with a little water or selters;
1 wine-glassful of port wine;
1 pony-glass of brandy (Martell);
½ glass of curaçao.
Fill the glass with fine ice; stir well with a spoon; ornament the top with grapes, oranges, etc., if in season; and serve with a straw.
This is one of the most popular summer drinks known in the South, and is very refreshing.

HOW TO MIX ABSINTHE.

(Use an absinthe glass.)

In preparing the above drink you must be particular and inquire, whether the customer desires it in the old French style or on the new, improved plan.

Mix as follows in a large bar or absinthe glass:—1 pony-glass of absinthe, place this into the large glass, take the top part of the absinthe glass, which has the shape of a bowl, with a small, round hole in the bottom, fill this with finely shaved ice and water; then raise the bowl up high, and let the water run or drip into the glass containing the absinthe; the color of the absinthe will show when to stop; then pour into the large glass, and serve.

None but genuine absinthe should be used, which you can easily recognize by the color in mixing, as it will turn to a milk color and look cloudy, which the domestic article does not. This is what they call an old-style French absinthe.

AMERICAN STYLE OF MIXING ABSINTHE.

(Use a large bar glass.)

¾ glassful of fine ice;
6 or 7 dashes of gum syrup;
1 pony-glass of absinthe;
2 wine-glasses of water.

Then shake the ingredients, until the outside of the shaker is covered with ice; strain it into a large bar glass, and serve. The way this is mixed it is more pleasant to drink than the French style. The Americans are not in the habit of drinking absinthe like the French are, but a drink of it occasionally will hurt nobody.

This is what they call American or frozen absinthe.

ITALIAN STYLE OF MIXING ABSINTHE.

(Use a large bar glass.)

1 pony-glass of absinthe;
2 or 3 lumps of broken ice;
2 or 3 dashes of maraschino;
½ pony-glass of anisette.

Take a small pitcher of ice water, and pour the water slowly into a large bar glass containing the mixture; stir with a spoon, and serve.

This is a very pleasant way of drinking absinthe, as it promotes the appetite; it is especially recommended before meals.

GERMAN OR SWISS STYLE OF MIXING ABSINTHE.

(Use a large bar glass.)

The Germans and the Swiss have the simplest way of drinking absinthe that I met with in my travels through Europe. If a person goes to a café, or bar room (as we call it), and asks for absinthe, the bartender or waiter puts a pony-glass of absinthe into a large tumbler and sends this and a pitcher of water to the customer, who helps himself to as much as he desires, and there is no mixing or fixing up about it. I consider this a very simple style of drinking absinthe, as it tastes just as good to them and answers the purpose.

The very latest of all in drinking absinthe at the present time can be seen in the city of Paris and other cities of France. When a gentleman comes into a café and sits down and gives his order to the waiter for his absinthe, the latter puts before the customer the bottle of absinthe as well as a bottle of anisette, a piece of loaf sugar, a pair of tongues to hold the sugar, and a decanter or pitcher of ice water; the customer puts his absinthe into the large absinthe glass, and as much of it as he desires; then places the sugar tongues across the top of the glass, and the sugar on top of the tongues; pours a few drops of anisette on top of his sugar, according to his taste; and he then fills up the absinthe glass with ice water until the absinthe has a milky, cloudy appearance.

GOLDEN FIZZ.
(Use a large bar glass.)

¾ table-spoonful of sugar;
2 or 3 dashes of lemon juice;
1 wine-glass of whiskey or Tom gin (according to the customer's taste);
1 egg (the yolk only);
¾ glassful of finely shaved ice.

Shake up well in a shaker; strain it into a good-sized fizz-glass; fill up the glass with syphon, vichy, or selters waters; mix well with a spoon, and serve.

This drink will suit old Harry, and is very delicious in the hot season. It must be drank as soon as mixed, else it will lose its flavor.

FAIVRE'S POUSSE CAFE.
(Use a sherry wine glass.)

$1/3$ glassful of Benedictine;
$1/3$ glassful of curaçao (red);
$1/3$ glassful of "Kirschwasser" or brandy (Martell);
2 or 3 drops of bitters (Boker's genuine only).

Attention must be paid to prevent the different colors from running into each other; they should be kept separate. Use a sherry-glass in pouring out the liquors, as it has a better appearance and works quicker.

WHISKEY CRUSTA.
(Use a large bar glass.)

Take a nice, clean lemon, of the same size as that of your wine-glass, cut off both ends, and peel it in the same way as you would peel an apple; put the lemon peel into the wine-glass, so that it will line the entire inside of the glass; then dip the edge of the glass and lemon peel in pulverized sugar.

The mixture is as follows:

½ pony-glass of orchard syrup;
1 or 2 dashes of bitters (Boker's genuine only);
1 dash of lemon juice;
2 dashes of maraschino;
½ glass of fine shaved ice;
¾ wine glass of whiskey;

Mix well with a spoon, strain it into the wine glass containing the lemon peel, ornament it with a little fruit, and serve.

MILK PUNCH.
(Use a large bar glass.)

¾ tablespoonful sugar;
$1/_3$ glass of fine ice;
1 wine glass of brandy; Martel;
½ wine glass of St. Croix rum;

Fill the glass with rich milk, shake the ingredients together, strain into a fancy bar glass, grate a little nutmeg on top and serve.

Bartenders must understand that these prescriptions for mixed drinks are strictly and exclusively first-class; therefore, if a bartender works in a place which is not first-class, and is not getting a high price for his drinks, he must use his own judgment about the ingredients, in order not to sell his drinks without profit. For instance where I say brandy in this mixed drink, whiskey would have to be taken in place of it, and where the prescription calls for St. Croix rum, take Medford rum, etc. These would be proper ingredients where a low price is charged for a Milk Punch.

This illustration will answer for all other drinks.

KNICKERBEIN.

(Use a sherry wine glass.)

$1/_3$ sherry wine glass vanilla;
1 fresh egg (the yolk only); cover the egg with benedictine;
$1/_3$ sherry wine glass of Kirschwasser or cognac;
4 to 6 drops bitters (Boker's genuine only).

Particular care must be taken with the above drink, the same as with Pousse Café, to prevent the liquors from running into each other, so that the yoke of the egg and the different liquors are kept separated from each other.

SELTERS LEMONADE.

(Use a large bar glass.)

1½ tablespoonfuls of sugar;
4 to 6 dashes of lemon juice;
4 or 5 small lumps of broken ice

Then fill the glass up with syphon selters, stir up well with a spoon and serve.

If customers desire to have the imported selters waters, use that instead of the syphon selters.

In order to have the above drink mixed properly, you must not spare sugar or lemon juice, and if the customer requires his drink strained use a fancy goblet without putting in fruit.

VERMOUTH COCKTAIL.
(Use a large bar glass.)

¾ glass of shaved ice;
4 or 5 dashes of gum;
2 or 3 dashes of bitters (Boker's genuine only);
1 wine glass of vermouth;
2 dashes of maraschino;

Stir up well with a spoon; strain it into a cocktail glass, twist a piece of lemon peel on top, and put a cherry in if required, and serve.

SAUTERNE COBBLER.
(Use a large bar glass.)

½ tablespoonful of sugar;
½ wine glass orchard syrup;
¼ wine glass of water or selters; dissolve well with a spoon;
Fill the glass with fine shaved ice;
1½ wine glass Sauterne wine; stir up well, ornament with grapes, oranges, pineapple, berries, etc., in a tasty manner, and serve with a straw.

SANTINAS POUSSE CAFE.
(Use a sherry wine glass.)

$1/3$ wine glass of maraschino;
$1/3$ wine glass of curaçoa (red);
$1/3$ wine glass of French brandy; and serve.

This drink is generally indulged in after partaking of a cup of black coffee, and care must be taken to prevent the different liquors from running into each other, as the proper appearance has a great deal to do with it.

Use a sherry glass in pouring in the different cordials.

BRANDY FIX.
(Use a large bar glass.)

½ tablespoonful of sugar;
2 or 3 dashes of lemon or lime juice;
½ pony glass of pineapple syrup;
1 or 2 dashes of chartreuse (green), dissolved well with a little water or selters;
Fill up the glass with shaved ice;
1 wine glass of brandy (Martell).
Stir up with a spoon, and ornament the top in a tasteful manner (with grapes and berries, in season), and serve with a straw.

CLARET PUNCH.
(Use a large bar glass.)

¾ tablespoonful of sugar;
1 squirt of selters;
Fill with ice;
½ dash of lemon juice, provided the claret wine is not too sour;
Fill the glass with claret wine, stir up well with a spoon; ornament with oranges, berries, pineapple, etc., in season, and serve.
This is a very popular summer drink, and is very cooling in hot weather.

FANCY BRANDY SMASH.
(Use a large bar glass.)

½ tablespoonful of sugar;
¼ wine glass of water or selters;
3 or 4 sprigs of fresh mint; dissolve well;
½ glass of shaved ice;
1 wine glass of brandy (Martell);
Stir up well with a spoon, strain it into a fancy bar glass, and ornament it with a little fruit in season, and serve. (See illustration, plate No. 9.)

SHERRY WINE PUNCH.
(Use a large bar glass.)

½ wine glass of orchard syrup;
1 dash of lemon juice;
Fill the glass with fine shaved ice;
1½ wine glass of sherry wine;
Stir up well with a spoon ornament with grapes, oranges, pineapples and berries; top it off with a little claret wine, and serve with a straw.

This is a very delicious summer drink and is well known.

BRANDY FLIP.
(Use a large bar glass.)

1 fresh egg;
¾ tablespoonful of sugar;
¾ glass of shaved ice
1 wine glass full of brandy (Martell);
Shake the above ingredients well in a shaker, strain into a flip or other fancy bar glass, and grate a little nutmeg on top, and serve.

WHISKEY JULEP.
(Use a large bar glass.)

¾ tablespoonful of sugar;
½ wine glass of water or selters;
3 or 4 sprigs of fresh mint dissolve well until all the essence of the mint is extracted;
Fill up the glass with fine shaved ice
1 wine glass full of whiskey.
Stir up well with a spoon and ornament this drink with mint, oranges, pineapples, and berries in a tasty manner; sprinkle a little sugar on top of it; dash with Jamaica rum, and serve.

PORT WINE PUNCH.
(Use a large bar glass.)

½ tablespoonful of orchard syrup
1 glass full of fine ice;
½ tablespoonful of sugar;
1 or 2 dashes of lemon juice;
½ wine glass full of water dissolve well with the sugar and lemon;
Fill up the glass with port wine.
Mix well with a spoon and ornament the top with grapes, oranges, pineapple and berries, and serve with a straw.

TIP-TOP PUNCH.
(Use a large bar glass.)

3 or 4 lumps of broken ice;
1 pony glass of brandy (Martell);
1 piece of loaf sugar;
1 or 2 slices of orange
1 or 2 slices of pineapple;
2 or 3 drops of lemon juice;
Fill up the balance with champagne (Piper Heidsieck).
Mix well with a spoon, dress up the top with fruits in season, and serve with a straw.
This drink is only mixed where they have champagne on draught, as mentioned in other receipts.

MEDFORD RUM SOUR.
(Use a large bar glass.)

½ tablespoonful of sugar;
3 or 4 dashes of lemon juice;
1 squirt of syphon selters, dissolved well
1 wine glass of Medford rum;
Fill ¾ of the glass with ice.

Stir well with a spoon strain into a sour glass, ornament with fruit, etc., and serve.

This is an old Boston drink, and has the reputation of being cooling and pleasant.

TOM COLLINS.

(Use an extra large bar glass.)

¾ tablespoonful of sugar;
3 or 4 dashes of lime or lemon juice;
3 or 4 pieces of broken ice;
1 wine glass of Old Tom gin (genuine only);
1 bottle of plain soda water.

Mix well with a spoon, remove the ice, and serve.

Attention must be paid not to let the foam of the soda water spread over the glass; this drink must be drank as soon as mixed in order not to let it get stale and lose its flavor.

THE OLD DELAWARE FISHING PUNCH.

(Use a large bar glass.)

1 tablespoonful of sugar;
1 or 2 dashes of lemon juice;
1 or 2 dashes of lime juice; dissolve well in a little water or a squirt of seltzer;
Fill up the glass with fine ice;
1 wine glass of St. Croix rum;
1 pony glass of old brandy (Martell).

Stir up well with a spoon, dress the top with fruit in season, and serve with a straw.

This drink can also be put up in bottles for the fisherman to take along, so that he will lose no time while fishing.

BOWL OF EGG NOGG FOR A NEW YEAR'S PARTY.

In regard to this drink the bartender must use his own judgment and use the proportions in accordance to the quantity to be made. For a three-gallon bowl, mix as follows:

2½ lbs. of fine pulverized sugar;
20 fresh eggs; have the yolks separated; beat as thin as water, and add the yolks of the eggs into the sugar and dissolve by stirring;
.2 quarts of good old brandy (Martell);
1½ pints of Jamaica rum;
2 gallons of good rich milk.

Mix the ingredients well with a ladle, and stir continually while pouring in the milk, to prevent it from curdling; then beat the whites of the eggs to a stiff froth and put this on top of the mixture; then fill a bar glass with a ladle, put some small pieces of the egg froth on top, grate a little nutmeg over it, and serve.

This will give you a splendid Egg Nog for all New Year's callers.

GIN FIZZ.
(Use a large bar glass.)

½ tablespoonful of sugar;
3 or 4 dashes of lemon juice;
½ glass of shaved ice;
1 wine glass of Old Tom gin.

Stir up well with a spoon, strain it into a large-sized bar glass, fill up the balance with vichy or selters water, mix well and serve.

Bear in mind that all drinks called Fizz's must be drank as soon as handed out, or the natural taste of the same is lost to the customer.

APPLE JACK SOUR.
(Use a large bar glass.)

½ tablespoonful of sugar;
2 or 3 dashes of lemon juice;
1 squirt of syphon selters water; dissolve well;
¾ glass of fine shaved ice;
1 wine glass of old cider brandy or what they call apple jack.

Stir up with a spoon, strain it into a sour glass, and ornament it with a little fruit, and serve.

This has always been a very fashionable drink with Jersey people.

EAST INDIA COCKTAIL.
(Use a large bar glass.)

Fill the glass with shaved ice;
1 teaspoonful of curaçoa (red)
1 teaspoonful of pineapple syrup;
2 or 3 dashes of bitters (Boker's genuine only);
2 dashes of maraschino;
1 wine glass full of brandy (Martell).

Stir up with a spoon, strain into a cocktail glass, putting in a cherry or medium-sized olive, twist a piece of lemon peel on top, and serve.

This drink is a great favorite with the English living in the different parts of East India.

HOW TO MIX TOM AND JERRY.
(Use a punch bowl for the mixture.)

Use eggs according to quantity. Before using eggs, be careful and have them fresh and cold; go to work and take two bowls, break up your eggs very carefully, without mixing the yolks with the whites, but have the whites in a separate bowl; take an egg-beater, and beat the whites of the eggs in such a manner that it becomes a stiff froth; add 1½ tablespoonfuls of sugar for each egg, and mix this thoroughly together, and then beat the yolks of the eggs until they are as thin as water; mix the yolks of the eggs with the whites and sugar together, until the mixture gets the consistency of a light batter, and it is necessary to stir the mixture up every little while to prevent the eggs from separating.

HOW TO DEAL OUT TOM AND JERRY.
(Take either a Tom and Jerry mug, or a bar glass.)

2 tablespoonfuls of the above mixture;
1 wine glass of brandy (Martell);
1 pony glass of Jamaica rum;

Fill the mug or glass with hot water or hot milk, and stir up well with a spoon, then pour the mixture from one mug to the other three or four times until the above ingredients are thoroughly mixed, grate a little nutmeg on top, and serve.

WHISKEY COCKTAIL.
(Use a large bar glass.)

¾ glass of fine shaved ice;
2 or 3 dashes of gum syrup; very careful not to use too much;
1½ or 2 dashes of bitters (Boker's genuine only);
1 or 2 dashes of curaçoa;
1 wine glass of whiskey.

Stir up well with a spoon and strain it into a cocktail glass, putting in a cherry or a medium-sized olive, and squeeze a piece of lemon peel on top, and serve.

This drink is without doubt one of the most popular American drinks in existence.

PLATE No. 12.

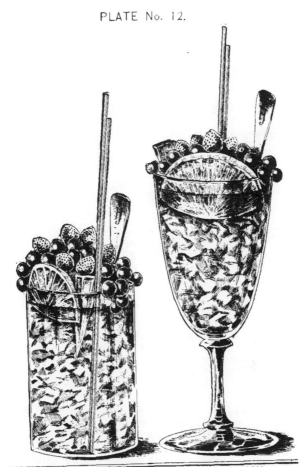

MISSISSIPPI PUNCH. CURACOA PUNCH.

Copyrighted, 1888.

LEMONADE.
(Use a large bar glass.)

1½ tablespoonful of sugar
6 to 8 dashes of lemon juice;
¾ glass filled with shaved ice;
Fill the balance with water; shake or stirr well; dress with fruit in season, in a tasteful manner, and serve with a straw.

To make this drink taste pleasant, it must be at all times strong; therefore take plenty of lemon juice and sugar.

WHISKEY SOUR
(Use a large bar glass.)

½ tablespoonful of sugar;
3 or 4 dashes of lemon juice;
1 squirt of syphon selter water, dissolve the sugar and lemon well with a spoon
Fill the glass with ice;
1 wine glass of whiskey:
Stir up well, strain into a sour glass;
Place your fruit into it, and serve.

BRANDY SCAFFA.
(Use a sherry glass.)

¼ sherry glass of raspberry syrup;
¼ sherry glass of maraschino;
¼ sherry glass of chartreuse (green);
Top it off with brandy (Martell) and serve.

This drink must be properly prepared to prevent the different colors from running into each other; each must appear separate; use a sherry glass for pouring out, as it has a better appearance and does the work much quicker.

CLARET AND CHAMPAGNE CUP A LA BRUNOW.

(Use a large punch bowl for a party of twenty.)

The following claret and champagne should from its excellence be called the Nectar of the Czar, as it is so highly appreciated in Russia, where for many years it has enjoyed a high reputation amongst the aristocracy of the Muscovite Empire.

Proportions.

3 bottles of claret;
2/3 pint of curaçoa;
1 pint of sherry;
1 pint of brandy (Martell);
2 wine glasses of ratafia of raspberries;
3 oranges and 1 lemon, cut in slices;
Some sprigs of green balm, and of borage;
2 bottles of German seltser water;
3 bottles of soda water;

Stir this together, and sweeten with capillaire pounded sugar until it ferments; let it stand one hour; strain it and ice it well; it is then fit for use; serve it in small glasses. The same for champagne cup, champagne (Piper Heidsick) instead of claret; noyan instead of ratafia. This quantity for an evening party of twenty persons, for a smaller number reduce the proportions.

PRUSSIAN GRANDEUR PUNCH.

(Use a large bowl.)

1½ lbs. of loaf sugar;
6 lemons, cut in slices;
1 gill of anisette;
1 bottle of Berlin kummel;
6 oranges, sliced;
1 bottle of kirschwasser;

½ gallon of water;
6 bottles of Nordhauser brantwein;
1 gill of curaçoa.

Stir up well with a punch ladle, and surround the bowl with ice, and serve in a wine glass.

JAPANESE COCKTAIL.
(Use a large bar glass.)

¾ glass of shaved ice;
2 or 3 dashes of orgeat syrup;
2 or 3 dashes of bitters (Boker's genuine only);
2 dashes of maraschino;
1 glass of eau celeste (Himmels Wasser).

Mix well with a spoon and strain it into a fancy cocktail glass, putting in a medium-sized olive, twist a piece of lemon peel on top, and serve.

BEEF TEA.
(Use a hot water glass.)

¼ teasponful of the best beef extract; fill the glass with hot water; stir up well with a spoon, and hand this to the customer, place pepper, salt and celery salt handy, and if the customer should require it, put in a small quantity of sherry wine or brandy, for which there should be an extra charge.

SARATOGA COCKTAIL.
(Use a large bar glass.)

¾ glass of fine shaved ice;
2 or 3 dashes of pineapple syrup;
2 or 3 dashes of bitters (Boker's genuine only);
2 or 3 dashes of maraschino (di Zara);
¾ glass of old brandy (Martell);

Mix well with a bar spoon and place 2 or 3 strawberries in a fancy cocktail glass, strain it, twist a piece of lemon peel over it, top it off with 1 squirt of champagne, and serve.

BRANDY DAISY.
(Use a large bar glass.)

½ tablespoonful of sugar;
2 or 3 dashes of lemon juice;
1 squirt of selters water, dissolve well with a spoon;
½ glass of chartreuse (yellow);
Fill up glass with fine ice;
1 glass of brandy (Martell);

Stir up well with a spoon, place the fruit into a fancy bar glass, strain the ingredients into it, and serve.

EMPIRE PUNCH.
(Use an extra large bowl.)

Rub the peel of 4 fine lemons, and also the peel of two oranges, until it has absorbed all the yellow part of the oil of the lemon and orange;

1½ lb of lump sugar;
1 pineapple, cut in slices;
12 fine oranges, cut in slices;
1 box of strawberries, which must be thoroughly cleaned;
2 bottles of apollinaris water; mix the above ingredients well with a ladle, and add
½ gill of maraschino;
½ gill of curaçoa;
½ gill of benedictine;
½ gill of Jamaica rum;
1 bottle brandy (Martell);
6 bottles of champagne (Piper Heidsieck);
4 bottles of Tokay wine;

2 bottles of Madeira;
4 bottles of Chateau Lafitte;

And mix this well with a large ladle, then strain through a very fine sieve into a clean bowl and surround the bowl with ice, fill it up over the edge of the bowl, which will give it a beautiful appearance, and dress the edge with some leaves and fruit, and ornament the punch in a fancy manner with grapes, oranges, pineapple and strawberries in season.

EGG LEMONADE.
(Use a large bar glass.)

1 fresh egg;
½ tablespoonful of sugar;
7 or 8 dashes of lemon juice;
¾ glass of fine ice.

Fill up the balance with water; shake up in a shaker, until all the ingredients are well mixed; then strain into a large bar glass, and serve.

This is a delicious summer drink of Americans, and is also fancied by the ladies; no fruits should be used for this drink.

WHISKEY COBBLER.
(Use a large bar glass.)

½ tablespoonful of sugar;
1½ teaspoonfuls of pineapple syrup;
½ wine glass of water or selters, dissolve well with a spoon;
Fill up the glass with fine ice;
1 wine glass of whiskey;

Stir up well with a spoon, and ornament on top with grapes, pineapple and berries in season, and serve with a straw.

SHERRY AND EGG.

(Use a whiskey glass.)

In preparing the above drink, place a small portion of sherry wine into the glass, barely enough to cover the bottom, to prevent the egg from sticking to the glass, then break a fresh ice-cold egg into it, hand this out to the customer and also the bottle of sherry wine to help himself.

It is always proper to ask the customer whether he wishes the yolk or the entire egg.

MAY WINE PUNCH.

(Use a large punch bowl.)

Take one or two bunches of (Waldmeister) Woodruff, and cut it up in two or three lengths, place it into a large bar glass, and fill up the balance with French brandy, cover it up and let it stand for two or three hours, until the essence of the Woodruff is thoroughly extracted; cover the bottom of the bowl with loaf sugar, and pour from

4 to 6 bottles of plain soda water over the sugar;

Cut up 6 oranges in slices;

½ pineapple, and sufficient berries and grapes;

8 bottles of rhine or moselle wine;

1 bottle of champagne (Piper Heidsieck);

Then put your Woodruff and brandy, etc., into the bowl, and stir up with a ladle, and you will have $2\frac{1}{2}$ to 3 gallons of excellent May wine punch.

Surround the bowl with ice, serve in a wine glass in such a manner that each customer will get a piece of all of the fruits contained in the punch.

HOT SPICED RUM.
(Take a hot water glass.)

1 or 2 lumps of loaf sugar;
$\frac{1}{2}$ teaspoonful of mixed allspice; dissolve with a little hot water;
1 wine glass of Jamaica rum;

Fill up the balance of the glass with hot water, mix well and grate a little nutmeg on top, and serve.

If the customer requires a small portion of butter in the above drink you should use only that which is perfectly fresh, as butter is very desirable in cases of sore throats and colds, and sometimes a little batter of the Tom and Jerry is required in this hot drink.

EGG MILK PUNCH.
(Use a large bar glass.)

1 fresh egg;
$\frac{3}{4}$ tablespoonful of sugar;
$\frac{1}{4}$ glass of fine shaved ice;
1 wine glass of brandy (Martell);
1 pony of St. Croix rum;

Fill up the balance with good milk, shake the ingredients well together until they become a stiff cream; strain into a large bar glass; grate a little nutmeg on top, and serve.

ST. CROIX CRUSTA.
(Use a large bar glass.)

Take a nice clean lemon, the size as your wine glass, cut off both ends, and peel it the same as you would an apple; put the lemon peel in the glass, so that it will line the entire inside of the glass, dip the edge of the glass and lemon peel in pulverized sugar and mix as follows:

3 or 4 dashes of orchard syrup;
1 dash bitters (Boker's genuine only);

½ glass of fine ice;
1 small dash of lemon juice;
2 dashes of maraschino;
1 wine glass of St. Croix rum;
Mix well with a spoon and strain into a wine glass, dress with small pieces of pineapple and strawberries, and serve.

SODA COCKTAIL.
(Use a large bar glass.)

4 or 5 lumps of broken ice;
5 or 6 dashes of bitters (Boker's genuine only);
1 or 2 slices of orange;
Fill up the glass with lemon soda water and place a teaspoon filled with sugar on top of the glass for the customer to put it in himself.
Do not let the foam of the soda spread over the glass in mixing the drink.

OLD STYLE WHISKEY SMASH.
(Use an extra large whiskey glass.)

¼ tablespoonful of sugar;
½ wine glass of water;
3 or 4 sprigs of mint, dissolve well, in order to get the essence of the mint;
Fill the glass with small pieces of ice;
1 wine glass of whiskey;
Put in fruit in season, mix well, place the strainer in the glass and serve.

JOHN COLLINS
(Use an extra large bar glass.)

¾ tablespoonful of sugar;
2 or 3 dashes of lemon juice;
2 dashes of lime juice;
4 or 5 small lumps of ice;
1 wineglassful of Holland gin;

Pour in a bottle of plain soda, mix up well, remove the ice and serve.

Care must be taken not to let the foam of the soda water run over the glass while pouring it in. This drink must be taken as soon as mixed or it will loose its flavor.

BLUE BLAZER.
(Use a large mug with a handle to it.)

½ pony glass of honey or rock candy;
½ wine glass syrup;
1 wine glass of whiskey (Scotch).

Mix well with a little hot water and put it over the fire and have it boiled up; set the liquid on fire, and take it quick and pour it from one mug to the other, pour it so about three or four times in long streams, until it is well mixed; grate a little nutmeg on top; this will have the appearance of a continual stream of fire. Attention must be paid to prevent the fire from spreading over your hands; pour it into a large size hot water glass, put a slice of lemon into it, and serve.

This is a very elegant drink in cold weather and has a wonderful effect of healing an old cold, especially when the party goes to bed soon after drinking it.

ALE SANGAREE.
(Use a large bar glass.)

1 tablespoonful of sugar;
½ wine glass of water, dissolve with a spoon.

Fill up the balance with ale, grate a little nutmeg on top, and serve.

It is customary to ask the customer if he desires old, new or mixed ale; if he desires new ale, you must prevent the foam from running over the glass; attention must also be paid to the temperature of the ale, so as to have it not too cold or too warm.

GENERAL HARRISON EGG NOGG.
(Use a large bar glass.)

1 fresh egg;
¼ tablespoonful of sugar;
3 or 4 lumps of ice;
Fill the glass with cider;
Shake well; strain it into a large bar glass; grate a little nutmeg on top and serve.

The above drink is a very pleasant one, and is popular throughout the Southern part of the country, and it is not intoxicating.

It is proper to use the very best quality of cider, as by using poor cider it is impossible to make this drink palatable.

ST. CROIX RUM PUNCH.
(Use a large bar glass.)

1 tablesponful of sugar;
3 or 4 dashes of lime or lemon juice;
½ wine glass of water or squirt of seltzer, dissolved well with a spoon;
¼ pony glass of Jamaica rum;
1 wine glass of St. Croix rum;
Fill up with fine shaved ice;
Mix well with a spoon, ornament with fruit in season, and serve with a straw.

This is a very cooling and pleasant drink in the hot season, providing you don't use poor rum.

SODA LEMONADE.
(Use a large bar glass.)

1 tablespoonful of sugar;
6 to 8 dashes of lemon juice;
3 or 4 lumps of broken ice;
1 bottle of plain soda water;

Stir up well with a spoon, remove the ice and serve.

Open the soda beneath the counter, to avoid squirting part of it over the customer; fruit should not be used in this drink.

RHINE WINE COBBLER.
(Use a large bar glass.)

1½ tablespoonfuls of sugar;
1½ wine glass of water or a squirt of syphon selters or vichy; dissolve well with a spoon;
1½ wine glasses of Rhine wine;
Fill the glass with shaved ice.

Stir up well with a spoon; ornament with grapes, orange, pineapple, strawberries, if in season, in a tasteful manner, and serve with a straw.

This is a fashionable German drink, and tastes very pleasant.

KIRSCHWASSER PUNCH.
(Use a large bar glass.)

½ tablespoonful of sugar;
1 or 2 dashes of lemon or lime juice;
3 or 4 dashes of chartreuse (yellow);
Dissolve well with a little water or a squirt of seltzer;
Fill the glass with ice;
1½ wine glass of Kirschwasser.

Mix well with a spoon, ornament the top with fruit, in a tasteful manner, in season, and serve with a straw.

MULLED CLARET AND EGG.
(Use a large bar glass.)

1 tablespoonful of sugar;
1 teaspoonful of cloves and cinnamon mixed;
2 wine glasses of claret wine.
Pour this into a dish over the fire until boiling;

2 yolks of fresh eggs, beaten to a batter with a little white sugar.

Pour the hot wine over the eggs, stirring continually while doing so, grate a little nutmeg on top, and serve. Do not stir the eggs into the wine, as this would spoil the drink; it is understood in mixing this drink that $\frac{1}{2}$ bottle of claret is used as a rule.

HOT APPLE TODDY.
(Use a hot apple toddy glass.)

In mixing this drink, an extra large hot-water glass must be used. Mix as follows:

$\frac{1}{2}$ medium-sized well roasted or baked apple

$\frac{1}{2}$ tablespoonful of sugar; dissolve well with a little hot water;

1 wine glass full of old apple jack.

Fill the balance with hot water, mix well with a spoon, grate a little nutmeg on top, and serve with a bar spoon.

If the customer desires the drink strained, use a fine strainer, such as used for milk punches; attention must be given while roasting the apples, that they are not overdone, but done in a nice and juicy manner; use only apples of the finest quality.

PORTER SANGAREE.
(Use a large bar glass.)

$\frac{1}{2}$ tablespoonful of sugar;

1 wine glass of water; dissolve the sugar well;

3 or 4 small pieces of broken ice;

Fill up the balance of the glass with porter; mix well with a spoon, remove the ice, and add a little more porter in order to fill the glass; grate a little nutmeg on top, and serve.

Do not let the foam of the porter spread over the glass.

HOT LEMONADE.
(Use a large bar glass.)

1 tablespoonful of sugar;
7 or 8 dashes of lemon juice;
Fill up the glass with hot water; stir up with a spoon, and serve.

It is always necessary to pour a little hot water into the glass at first and stir a little, to prevent the glass from cracking, and also place a little fine ice in a separate glass in case the the drink should be too hot; in order to make this drink palatable, sugar and lemon should not be spared.

ARF AND ARF.
(Use a large bar glass.)

The above is an old English drink, and has become quite a favorite in this country; it is mixed as follows:
½ glass of porter and the other half glass of ale.

But in this country it is mostly understood to use half old ale and half new ale mixed; the proper way is to ask how the customer desires it, and see that the drink is cold enough in summer time, but still not too cold.

ST. CROIX FIX.
(Use a large bar glass.)

½ tablespoonful of sugar;
2 or 3 dashes of lemon juice;
½ pony glass of pineapple syrup;
½ wine glass of water; dissolve well with a spoon;
Fill up the glass with ice;
1 wine glass of St. Croix rum.

Stir up well; ornament the top with fruit in season, in a tasteful manner, and serve with a straw.

JERSEY COCKTAIL.
(Use a large bar glass.)

¼ tablespoonful of sugar;
3 or 4 lumps of broken ice;
3 or 4 dashes of bitters (Boker's genuine only);
1 wine glass of good cider.

Mix well and strain into a cocktail glass, putting in a cherry or medium-sized olive, and twist a piece of lemon peel on top and serve.

This is a favorable drink with Jersey people.

ORANGE LEMONADE.
(Use a large bar glass.)

1 tablespoonful of sugar;
1 dash of lemon juice, squeeze out the juice of 1 or 2 oranges.

Fill the glass with shaved ice.

Fill the balance with water, shake or stir well and dress the top with fruit in season, in a tasteful manner, and serve with a straw.

This is a very delicious summer drink.

BISHOP.
(Use a large bar glass.)

1 tablespoonful of sugar;
2 dashes of lime or lemon juice.
½ orange squeezed into it;
½ wine glass of water, or syphon selters, or Vichy, dissolve well;
¾ of a glass of fine shaved ice;
Fill the glass with Burgundy;

Flavor with a few drops of Jamaica rum, stir up well with a spoon; dress the top with a little fruit and serve with a straw.

PLATE No. 13.

Danziger Goldwasse.

Yolk of a fresh cold Egg.

Chartreuse (yellow).

GOLDEN SLIPPER.

MARTINE COCKTAIL.

Copyrighted, 1888.

BRANDY FIZZ.

(Use a large bar glass.)

½ tablespoonful of sugar;
3 or 4 dashes of lemon juice;
¾ of a glass of fine ice;
1 wine glass of brandy (Martell);

Mix well with a spoon, strain into a fizz or sour glass, fill with vichy or selters water, and serve.

CHAMPAGNE VELVET.

(Use a large-sized goblet.)

For a large party, 1 quart bottle of champagne and a bottle of Irish porter must be opened; for a small party, 1 pint of champagne, 1 bottle of Irish porter; it is the bartender's duty to inquire what brand of wine the customer desires. Fill the glass half full with porter, the balance with champagne (Piper Heidsieck); stir up with a spoon slowly, and you have what is called champagne velvet, because it will make you feel within a short time as fine as silk.

It is rather an expensive drink, but a good one.

BURNT BRANDY AND PEACH.

(Use a small bar glass.)

This drink is a very popular one in the Southern States, where it is frequently used as a cure for diarrhea.

1 wine glass of cognac (Martell);
½ tablespoonful of white sugar, burned in a saucer or plate;
2 or 3 slices of dried peaches;

Place the dried fruit into a glass and pour the liquor over them; grate a little nutmeg on top and serve.

RHINE WINE AND SELTERS.
(Use a large wine glass.)

The bartender's attention is called to the fact that when a customer calls for Rhine wine and selters water, he desires a larger portion of wine than of selters, and, if he should call for selters and wine, he desires more selters than wine; it is understood, in serving wine and selters, the imported selters must be used, the artificial selters will spoil the wine and destroy its flavor; attention must be paid that both the wine and the selters are continually kept on ice.

This is a favorite drink with German people and preferred by them in many cases to lemonade.

IMPERIAL BRANDY PUNCH.
(For a party of twenty.)

4 quarts of German imported selters water;
3 quarts of brandy (Martell);
1 pint of Jamaica rum;
1½ pound of white sugar;
Juice of 6 lemons;
3 oranges sliced;
1 pinapple, pared and cut up;
1 gill of curaçoa;
2 gills of raspberry syrup;
Ice and berries in season;

Mix well together in a large bowl, and you will have a splendid punch.

If not sweet enough, add more sugar.

BRANDY AND SODA.
(Use a large bar glass.)

3 or 4 lumps of broken ice;
1 wine glass of brandy (Martell);
1 bottle of plain soda-water;

Mix well with a spoon, but attention must be paid not to let the mixture spread over the glass.

This is a delicious drink in summer and fancied very much by English people, and is also called Brandy Split by them.

CLARET COBBLER.

(Use a large bar glass or goblet.)

1 tablespoonful of orchard syrup;
½ tablespoonful of sugar;
¼ of an orange;
1 squirt of selters water; dissolve well with a spoon; fill with fine shaved ice;
1½ wine glass of good claret wine;

Stir well with a spoon, and ornament with slices of oranges, pineapple, lemon, etc., in a tasteful manner, and serve with a straw.

COLUMBIA SKIN.

(Use a small bar glass.)

1 teaspoonful of sugar, dissolve well with a little water;
1 slice of lemon;
2 or 3 pieces of broken ice;
1 wine glass of Medford rum;

Stir up well with a spoon; grate a little nutmeg on top and serve.

This drink is called Columbia Skin by the Boston people.

RASPBERRY SHRUB.
(Use a bowl for mixing.)

1 quart of vinegar;
3 quarts of ripe raspberries;

After standing a day, strain it, adding to each pint a pound of sugar, and skim it clear while boiling about half an hour.

Put a wine glass of brandy to each pint of the shrub when cool.

2 spoonfuls of this mixed with a tumbler of water is an excellent drink in warm weather and during a fever season.

CLARET CUP FOR A PARTY.
(Use a bowl for mixing.)

8 to 12 pieces of lump sugar;
1 bottle of Apollinaris water;
2 lemons, cut in slices;
2 oranges cut in slices;
½ pineapple, cut in slices;
2 wine glasses of maraschino;

Mix well with a ladle, place this into your vessel or tin dish filled with ice, then, when the party is ready to call for it, add:

4 bottles of very fine claret;
1 bottle of champagne (Piper Heidsieck), or any other sparkling wine;

Mix thoroughly and place sufficient berries on top and serve it into a fancy wine glass, and you will have an elegant Claret Cup.

CRIMEAN CUP À LA MARMORA.
(Use a bowl for mixing.)

1 pint of orgeat syrup;
½ pint of cognac brandy (Martell);
¼ pint of maraschino;

¼ pint of Jamaica rum;
1 bottle champagne (Piper Heidsieck);
1 bottle soda-water;
3 ounces of sugar;
2 lemons, cut in slices;
2 oranges, cut in slices;
A few slices of pineapple;

Stir up well with a spoon or ladle, then place it into your dish filled with ice, and serve.

BRANDY STRAIGHT.
(Use a whiskey glass.)

Hand out the glass with the bottle of brandy (Martell) to the customer, also a glass of ice water; as brandy is never kept on ice, the bartender should put a piece of ice in the glass; it is not pleasant to drink when warm; do the same with all other liquors that are not kept on ice.

GIN AND CALAMUS.
(Use a whiskey glass.)

In preparing this drink, take 3 or 4 long pieces of calamus root, cut it in small pieces and put into an empty bottle; fill up the bottle with gin, and let it draw sufficiently to get all the essence of the calamus into the gin.

In serving this drink, hand out the whiskey glass, and the bottle with the gin and calamus mixture, to let the customer help himself.

If the mixture in the bottle should be too strong for the customer, let him add plain gin to suit his taste.

MILK AND SELTERS.

(Use a medium-sized bar glass.)

In serving this drink, which is strictly temperance, it is proper for the bartender to half fill the glass with selters, and the rest with milk; if it is done otherwise, you will have nothing but foam in your glass, which would cause delay if a party has to be attended to.

BRANDY AND GINGER ALE.

(Use a large bar glass.)

2 or 3 lumps of broken ice;
1 wine glass of brandy (Martell);
1 bottle of good ginger ale;

Mix well together; particular attention must be paid when pouring the ginger ale into the other mixtures, not to let the foam run over the glass, and it is proper to ask the customer whether he desires imported or domestic ale; the imported being the best to use, as it mixes better and will give better satisfaction than the domestic.

BLACK STRIPE.

(Use a large bar glass.)

1 wine glass of Jamaica or St. Croix rum;
1 tablespoonful of molasses;

This drink can be made either in summer or winter; if in the former season, mix one tablespoonful of water and cool with shaved ice; if in the latter, fill up the glass with boiling water; use only the best New Orleans molasses, and grate a little nutmeg on top.

ORGEAT LEMONADE.
(Use a large bar glass.)

1½ wine glass of orgeat syrup;
½ tablespoonful of sugar;
6 to 8 dashes of lemon juice;
¾ glass of shaved ice;
Fill the glass with water;

Mix up well and ornament with grapes, berries, etc., in season, in a tasteful manner, and serve with a straw.

This is a fine drink in warm climates.

SOLDIERS' CAMPING PUNCH.

Boil a large kettle of strong black coffee; take a large dish and put 4 pounds of lump sugar into it; then pour 4 bottles of brandy (Martell) and 2 bottles of Jamaica rum over the sugar, and set it on fire, let the sugar dissolve and drop into the black coffee; stir this well, and you will have a good hot punch for soldiers on guard.

SARATOGA BRACE UP.
(Use a large bar glass.)

1 small tablespoonful of white sugar;
2 or 3 dashes of bitters (Boker's genuine only);
2 or 3 dashes of lemon juice;
1 dash of lime juice;
2 dashes of absinthe;
1 fresh egg;
¾ glass of brandy (Martell);
½ glass shaved ice;

Shake this up thoroughly in a shaker, strain it into a large size fancy bar glass, and fill with syphon Vichy or Apollinaris water and serve.

SHERRY WINE AND ICE.
(Use a whiskey glass.)

1 or 2 lumps of broken ice.

Place a bar spoon into the glass, hand this out with the bottle of sherry wine, and let the customer help himself.

If a hotel, restaurant, or café is attached to the establishment, and the customer should call for such drink at the table, it is the bartender's duty to fill the glass with sherry wine, and not send the bottle to the table, unless requested to do so.

But the proper style of all is to have your sherry wine or any other kind of wines, such as ports, sherries, Madeira, etc., in a small one-drink decanter.

THE AMERICAN CHAMPAGNE CUP.
(Use a large punch bowl for a party of forty.)

2 wine glasses of pineapple syrup;
4 to 6 sprigs of green balm;
1 quart of curaçoa (red);
1 pint of chartreuse (green);
1 quart of fine old brandy or cognac (Martell);
1 quart of Tokay wine;
4 bottles of Apollinaris water;
6 oranges, cut in slices;
2 lemons, cut in slices;

Stir up well together, let it stand two hours, strain it into another bowl and add:

$\frac{1}{4}$ pineapple cut in slices;
$\frac{1}{2}$ box of strawberries;
6 bottles of champagne (Piper Heidsieck);

Place the bowl in the ice, and sweeten with a little sugar and let it ferment; stir up well and serve the same as American Claret Cup, and this will give satisfaction to any bon-ton party in America.

FINE LEMONADE FOR PARTIES.

(Use a punch bowl—1 gallon.)

Take the rind of 8 lemons;
Juice of 12 lemons;
2 pounds of loaf sugar;
1 gallon of boiling water;

Rub the rinds of the 8 lemons on the sugar until it has absorbed all the oil from them, and put it with the remainder of the sugar into a jug; add the lemon juice and pour the boiling water over the whole. When the sugar is dissolved, strain the lemonade through a piece of muslin, and, when cool, it will be ready for use.

The lemonade will be much improved by having the whites of 4 eggs beaten up with it. A larger or smaller quantity of this lemonade may be made by increasing or diminishing the quantity of the ingredients.

BRANDY SHRUB.

(Use bowl to make six quarts.)

4 pounds of loaf sugar, dissolve well with a bottle of plain soda-water.
2 quarts of old brandy (Martell);
3 quarts of sherry wine;
10 lemons.
Peel the rinds of 4 lemons;

Add the juice of the other 6 lemons and mix with brandy into the bowl; cover it close for 5 days, then add the sherry wine and sugar, strain through a bag and bottle it. This also applies to all the other shrubs.

PUNCH À LA FORD.
(For bottling.)

3 dozen lemons;
1 pint cognac (Martell);
2 pounds of loaf sugar:
1 pint of Jamaica rum;
The lemons should have smooth rinds;

Peel the yellow rinds off quite thin with a sharp knife, place them in an earthen vessel; add the sugar and stir thoroughly for neary half an hour with a flat piece of wood to extract the essential oil. Pour on boiling water, and stir until the sugar is completely dissolved.

Cut and squeeze the lemon, straining the juice from the pits. Place the pits in a jug and pour boiling water upon them to obtain the mucilage in which they are enveloped. Pour $\frac{1}{2}$ of the lemon juice into the syrup, strain the water from the pits, and add it also to the syrup, taking care that the syrup is not too watery.

Next, add more sugar or lemon juice, to make the mixture according to taste.

Lastly, add and stir in the above amount of spirits into every 3 quarts of lemonade, and bottle.

This punch improves by age, if kept in a cool cellar.

ENGLISH BISHOP.
(Use a small punch bowl to make one quart.)

1 quart of port wine;
1 orange (stuck pretty well with cloves, the quantity being a matter of taste);

Roast the orange before a fire, and when sufficiently brown, cut in quarters, and pour over it a quart of port wine (previously made hot). Add sugar to taste, and let the mixture simmer over the fire for half an hour.

BRANDY AND GUM.
(Use a whiskey glass.)

3 or 4 dashes of gum;
1 or 2 pieces of broken ice;
Place a bar spoon into the glass and hand this with a bottle of brandy (Martell) to the customer to help himself.

When any other liquor is called for, it is served in the same manner.

WHISKEY AND CIDER.
(Use a whiskey glass.)

Hand the bottle of whiskey to the customer to help himself; fill up the glass with good apple cider, stir well with a spoon and serve, and you will have a very nice drink.

The author recommends good apple cider in preference to pear, or any other kind of fruit cider.

GIN AND MILK.
(Use a whiskey glass.)

Hand the bottle of gin, glass and spoon out to the customer to help himself; fill up the balance with good, rich, ice-cold milk, stir up with the spoon, and you will have a very nice drink.

SHANDY GAFF.
(Use a large bar glass or mug.)

Fill the glass half full of old ale or Bass ale, and the other half with Belfast ginger ale; stir up with a spoon and serve. This is an old English drink; proper attention must be taken in order to have the drink in the right temperature.

HOW TO SERVE A PONY GLASS OF BRANDY.
(Use a pony glass.)

In serving this drink, hand out the pony glass filled with brandy (Martell), also a whiskey glass, into which the brandy is emptied, a glass of ice water and a little separate ice to cool the brandy. The latest style of serving a pony of brandy is to place the pony at the edge of the counter, then take a whiskey tumbler upside down in the left hand, and place it over the pony glass of brandy, then reverse the glass as well as the pony glass containing the brandy, so as to have the stem of the pony glass on top and the brandy at the bottom of the whiskey glass, in order to be convenient for the customer. (See illustration, plate No. 2.)

HOT GIN SLING.
(Use a hot water glass.)

1 piece of loaf sugar, dissolve in a little water;
1 wine glass of Holland gin;
Fill up the balance with hot water;
Stir with a spoon, grate a little nutmeg on top, and serve. Add a slice of lemon if the customer desires it.

BOMBAY PUNCH.
(Use a large bowl.)

Rub the sugar over the lemons until it has absorbed all the yellow part of the skins of 6 lemons, then put in the punch bowl:
1 pound of loaf sugar;
2 bottles of imported selters water;
1 pineapple, cut into slices;
6 oranges, cut into slices;

1 box of strawberries;
2 lemons, cut up in slices; mix well with a spoon and add:
  4 bottles of champagne (Piper Heidsieck);
  1 or 2 bottles of brandy (Martell);
  1 bottle of pale sherry;
  1 bottle of Madeira wine;
  1 gill of maraschino;
Stir up well with a spoon or ladle, and surround the bowl with ice; serve it into a wine glass in such a manner, that each customer will have a piece of the above fruit.

GIN AND WORMWOOD.
(Use a small bar glass.)

Take six to eight sprigs of wormwood, put these in a quart bottle and fill up with Holland gin; leave this stand for a few days, until the essence of the wormwood is extracted into the gin. In handing out this, pour a little of the above into a small whiskey glass and hand it with the bottle of gin to the customer to help himself.

This drink is popular in the eastern part of the country, where the wormwood is used as a substitute for bitters.

SHERRY WINE EGG NOGG.
(Use a large bar glass.)

1 fresh egg;
½ tablespoonful of sugar;
Fill up the glass with fine ice;
1 pony glass of brandy (Martell);
1 wine glass of sherry wine;
Shake the above ingredients well, until they are thoroughly mixed together; strain it into a fancy wine glass, large enough to hold the mixture; grate a little nutmeg on top and serve.

MEDFORD RUM SMASH.
(Use a large bar glass.)

¼ tablespoonful of sugar;
½ wine glass of water, or squirt of seltzer;
2 or 3 sprigs of mint; dissolve well the sugar with the mint, so that the essence of the same is well extracted;
½ glass of fine ice;
1 wine glass of old Medford rum;

Stir well with a spoon, place the fruit into a sour glass and strain the above ingredients into it, and serve.

GIN FIX.
(Use a large bar glass.)

½ tablespoonful of sugar;
3 or 4 dashes of lime or lemon juice;
½ pony glass of pineapple syrup; dissolve well with a little water, or squirt of selters;
Fill up the glass with shaved ice;
1 wine glass of Holland gin;

Stir up well with a spoon, ornament the top with fruit in season, and serve with a straw.

COLD BRANDY TODDY.
(Use a whiskey glass.)

½ teaspoonful of sugar;
½ wine glass of water, disolve well with a spoon;
1 or 2 lumps of broken ice;
1 wine glass of brandy (Martell);

Stir up well, remove the ice, and serve.

It is proper to dissolve the sugar with the water, and hand the bottle of liquor, with glass and spoon, to the customer to help himself.

PLATE No. 14.

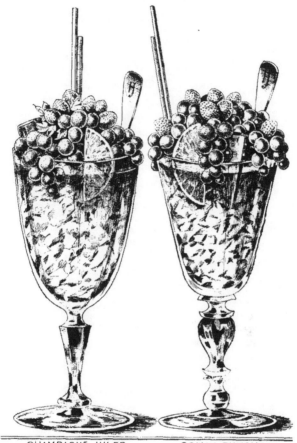

CHAMPAGNE JULEP.   ROMAN PUNCH.

Copyrighted, 1888.

BOTTLE OF COCKTAIL FOR PARTIES.

1 quart of good old whiskey, providing the bottle is large enough for the entire mixture;
1 pony glass of curaçoa (red);
1 wine glass of gum syrup (be careful in not using too much);
¾ pony glass of bitters (Boker's genuine only);
Mix this well by pouring it from one shaker into another, until it is thoroughly mixed; pour it into a bottle, and cork it; then put a nice label on it, and you will have an elegant bottle of cocktail.

CALIFORNIA SHERRY WINE COBBLER.
(Use a large bar glass.)

½ tablespoonful of sugar;
1 pony glass of pineapple syrup, dissolve well in a little water;
Fill the glass with ice;
1½ wineglassful of California sherry wine;
Stir up well with a spoon; ornament the top in a fancy manner with oranges, pineapple, and berries; top it off with a little old port wine, and serve with a straw.

ORCHARD PUNCH.
(Use a large bar glass.)

2 tablespoonfuls of orchard syrup;
2 or 3 dashes of lime or lemon juice;
½ pony glass of pineapple syrup, dissolve well with a little water or squirt of syphon, vichy, or selters;
Fill the glass with fine ice;
1 wineglassful of California brandy;
Mix well with a spoon, and ornament with grapes, oranges, pineapple, and berries in a tasteful manner; top off with a little port wine, and serve with a straw.

GIN AND TANSY.
(Use a whiskey glass.)

In preparing this drink, take a small bunch of tansy, and put it into an empty bottle or decanter; then fill it up with good old Holland gin, and let it draw sufficiently to get all the essence of the tansy into the gin. In serving this drink, hand out the glass and the bottle, with the gin and tansy mixture. If the mixture is too strong for the customer's taste, let him add a little more plain gin to it.

JAMAICA RUM SOUR.
(Use a large bar glass.)

½ tablespoonful of sugar;
2 or 3 dashes of lemon juice;
1 squirt of syphon selters, dissolve well with a spoon;
¾ glass of finely shaved ice;
1 wine glass of Jamaica rum;

Stir well with a spoon, strain it into a sour glass, ornament with fruit, and serve.

PORT WINE FLIP.
(Use a large bar glass.)

1 fresh egg;
½ tablespoonful of sugar;
¾ glass of shaved ice;
1 wine glass of port wine;

Shake well with a shaker, strain into a wine glass, grate a little nutmeg on top, and serve.

HOT ARRAC PUNCH.
(Use a hot water glass.)

1 or 2 pieces of lump sugar, dissolved in water;
3 or 4 drops of lemon juice;
¾ wine glass of arrac (Batavia);

Fill the glass with hot water, stir well with a spoon, grate a little nutmeg on top, and serve.

BRANDY SANGAREE.
(Use a small bar glass.)

1 or 2 lumps of ice;
½ wine glass of water;
½ tablespoonful of sugar;
1 glass of brandy (Martell);

Stir up well with a spoon, grate a little nutmeg on top, and serve; strain if desired.

GIN JULEP.
(Use a large bar glass.)

¾ tablespoonful of sugar;
3 or 4 sprigs of mint;
½ wine glass of water, dissolve well, until the essence of the mint is extracted, then remove the mint;
Fill up with fine ice;
1¼ wine glass of Holland gin;

Stir up well with a spoon, ornament it the same as you would mint julep, and serve.

HOT SCOTCH WHISKEY SLING.
(Use a hot water glass.)

1 piece of lump sugar;
¾ glass of hot water;
1 piece of lemon peel;
1 wine glass of Scotch whiskey;

Stir up well with a spoon, grate a little nutmeg on top, and serve.

SHERRY WINE AND BITTERS.
(Use a sherry wine glass.)

In preparing this drink, put in 1 small dash of bitters (Boker's genuine only), and twist or turn the glass in such a manner, that the bitters will line the entire inside of the glass; fill the glass up with sherry wine, and it will be mixed well enough to serve.

HOT MILK PUNCH.

(Use a large bar glass.)

1 tablespoonful of sugar;

¼ wine glass of Jamaica or St. Croix rum if required;

¾ wine glass of brandy (if desired use Jamaica rum instead of brandy);

Fill the glass with boiling hot milk;

Stir up well with a spoon, grate a little nutmeg over it, and serve.

In mixing this drink, you must never use the shaker; if hot milk is not handy, use a teaspoonful of condensed milk, and fill the balance with hot water; this will answer in place of hot milk.

GIN COCKTAIL.

(Use a large bar glass.)

Fill up the glass with ice;

2 or 3 dashes of gum syrup (be careful in not using too much);

2 or 3 dashes of bitters (Boker's genuine only);

1 dash of either curaçoa or absinthe;

1 wine glass of Holland gin;

Stir up well, strain into a fancy cocktail glass, putting in a cherry or medium-sized olive; squeeze a piece of lemon peel on top, and serve.

Whether curaçoa or absinthe is taken, depends on which the customer may desire.

TOM AND JERRY (cold).

(Use a Tom and Jerry mug, or a bar glass.)

This drink is prepared on the same principle as hot Tom and Jerry, with the exception of using cold water, or cold milk.

HOT WHISKEY.
(Use a hot whiskey glass.)

Place a bar spoon into the glass before pouring in hot water, to avoid cracking the glass, and have a separate glass filled with fine ice, which must be placed in a convenient position, so that if the customer finds his drink too hot, he can help himself to a little ice. The bartender should at all times handle the sugar with a pair of tongues. Mix as follows:

1 or 2 lumps of loaf sugar, with a little hot water to dissolve the sugar well;
1 wine glass of Scotch whiskey;

Fill the glass with hot water, then mix well; squeeze and throw in the lemon peel, grate a little nutmeg on top, and serve.

It is customary to use Scotch whiskey in preparing this drink, unless otherwise desired by the customer.

MEDFORD RUM PUNCH.
(Use a large bar glass.)

$\frac{3}{4}$ tablespoonful of sugar;
2 or 3 dashes of lemon juice, dissolve well with a little water, or squirt of syphon, vichy, or selters;
Fill the glass with finely shaved ice;
$1\frac{1}{2}$ wineglassful of Medford rum;

Flavor with a few drops of Jamaica rum, stir up well with a spoon, and dress the top with fruit in season in a tasteful manner, and serve with a straw.

WHISKEY FIZZ.
(Use a large bar glass.)

$\frac{1}{4}$ tablespoonful of sugar;
2 or 3 dashes of lemon juice, dissolve with a squirt of selters water;
Fill the glass with ice;
1 wine glass of whiskey;

Stir up well, strain into a good-sized fizz glass, fill the balance up with selters or vichy water, and serve.

This drink must be drank as soon as mixed, in order that it should not lose its flavor.

GIN SMASH.
(Use a large bar glass.)

½ tablespoonful of sugar;
2 or 3 sprigs of fresh mint, dissolve well with a little water until the essence of the mint is extracted;
½ glass of shaved ice;
1 wine glass of Holland gin;

Stir up well with a spoon, strain into a sour glass, ornament with fruit, and serve.

HOT LOCOMOTIVE.
(Use a large bar glass.)

1 yolk of a raw egg;
½ tablespoonful of sugar;
1 pony glass of honey, dissolve well with a spoon;
1½ wineglassful of Burgundy or claret;
½ pony glass of curaçoa;

Put all the ingredients into a dish, and place it over a fire until it boils up, then pour from one mug into the other (three or four times in succession), put a slice of lemon into it, sprinkle with a little cinnamon, and serve.

WHISKEY FIX.
(Use a large bar glass.)

½ tablespoonful of sugar;
2 or 3 dashes of lime or lemon juice, dissolve well with a little water;
½ pony glass of pineapple syrup;
¾ glass of shaved ice;
1 wine glass of whiskey;

Stir up well with a spoon, and ornament with grapes,

oranges, pineapple, and berries in a tasteful manner; serve with a straw.

HOT IRISH WHISKEY PUNCH.
(Use a hot water glass.)

1 or 2 lumps of loaf sugar;
1 squirt of lemon juice, dissolve in a little hot water;
1 wine glass of Irish whiskey;
Fill the glass with hot water, stir up well, put a slice of lemon into it, grate a little nutmeg on top, and serve.

STONE WALL.
(Use a large bar glass.)

$\frac{1}{4}$ tablespoonful of sugar;
3 or 4 lumps of ice;
1 wine glass of whiskey;
1 bottle of plain soda water;
Stir up well with a spoon, remove the ice, and serve.
This is a very cooling drink, and generally called for in the warm season.

STONE FENCE.
(Use a whiskey glass.)

1 wine glass of whiskey;
2 or 3 lumps of broken ice;
Fill the glass with cider, stir up well, and serve; as a rule it is left for the customer to help himself to the whiskey if he so desires.

SHERRY WINE SANGAREE.
(Use a whiskey glass.)

1 teaspoonful of sugar, dissolve well with a little water;
1 or 2 lumps of broken ice;
1 wine glass of sherry wine;
Stir up well with a spoon, remove the ice, **grate a** little nutmeg on top, and serve.

OLD TOM GIN COCKTAIL.
(Use a large bar glass.)

Fill the glass with finely shaved ice;
2 or 3 dashes of gum syrup;
1 or 2 dashes of bitters (Boker's genuine only);
1 or 2 dashes of curaçoa or absinthe if required;
1 wine glass of old Tom gin;

Stir up well with a spoon, strain into a cocktail glass, putting in a cherry or medium-sized olive if required.

Twist a piece of lemon peel on top, and serve.

GIN TODDY.
(Use a whiskey glass.)

½ teaspoonful of sugar, dissolve well in a little water;
1 or 2 lumps of broken ice;
1 wine glass of Holland gin;
Stir up well, and serve.

The proper way to serve this drink, is to dissolve the sugar with a little water, put the spoon and ice into the glass, and hand out the bottle of liquor to the customer to help himself.

WINE LEMONADE.
(Use a large bar glass.)

1 tablespoonful of sugar;
5 or 6 dashes of lemon juice;
Fill up the glass with fine ice;
1 wine glass of wine, either sherry, claret, or port wine, whichever may be desired;

Fill up the balance with water, shake well, and dress the top with fruit, then serve with a straw.

This is a favorite drink in Italy.

HOT RUM.
(Use a hot water glass.)

1 or 2 lumps of loaf sugar, dissolve with a little hot water;
1 wine glass of Jamaica rum;
Fill the balance with hot water, stir up well with a spoon, grate a little nutmeg on top, and serve.

The genuine Jamaica rum only should be used, in order to make this drink palatable.

SODA AND NECTAR.
(Use a large bar glass.)

3 or 4 dashes of lemon juice;
$\frac{3}{4}$ of a glass of water;
$\frac{1}{2}$ teaspoonful of bicarbonate of soda, with sufficient white sugar to sweeten nicely;

When mixed, put in the plain soda, stir well, and drink while in a foaming state.

This is an excellent morning drink to regulate the bowels.

GIN AND MOLASSES.
(Use a whiskey glass.)

Pour into the glass a small quantity of gin, in order to cover the bottom of it, then take 1 tablespoonful of New Orleans black molasses, and hand it with a bar spoon and the bottle of gin to the customer to help himself.

Hot water must be used to clean the glass afterwards, as it will be impossible to clean it in any other way.

FANCY BRANDY SOUR.
(Use a large bar glass.)

$\frac{1}{2}$ tablespoonful of sugar;
2 or 3 dashes of lemon juice;
1 squirt of syphon selters water, dissolve the sugar and lemon well with a spoon;

Fill up the glass with ice;
1 wine glass of brandy (Martell);
Stir up well, place the fruits into the fancy sour glass, strain the ingredients into it, and serve (see illustration, plate No. 11).

BALAKLAVA NECTAR.
(For a party of fifteen.)

Thinly peel the rind of half of a lemon, shred it fine, and put it in a punch bowl, add 4 tablespoonfuls of crushed sugar and the juice of 1 lemon;
1 gill of maraschino;
2 bottles of soda water (plain);
2 bottles of claret;
2 bottles of champagne (Piper Heidsieck);
Stir well together, and dress the top with fruits in season, then serve.

ENGLISH ROYAL PUNCH.
(Use a bowl for mixing for a small party.)

1 pint of hot, green tea;
½ pint of brandy (Martell);
½ pint of Jamaica rum;
1 wine glass of curaçoa;
1 wine glass of arrac;
Juice of 2 limes;
1 lemon, cut in slices;
½ pound of sugar;
Mix this thoroughly with a ladle, and add 4 eggs (the whites only), and drink this as hot as possible.

This composition is good enough for an emperor or a king, and the materials are admirably blended; the inebriating effects of the spirits being deadened by the tea, whilst the eggs soften the mixture, and destroy the acrimony of the acid and sugar. If the punch is too strong, add more green tea to taste; and if not hot enough, place the entire mixture over the fire, and have it heated, but not boiled; then serve.

SODA NEGUS.
(Use a small punch bowl; about one quart.)

1 pint of port wine;
12 lumps of white loaf sugar;
8 cloves;
Grated nutmeg, sufficient to fill a small tea spoon;

Put the above ingredients into a thoroughly clean sauce pan, warm and stir them well, but do not suffer it to boil; upon the warm wine empty a bottle of plain soda water. This makes a delicious and refreshing drink.

BOTTLED VELVET.
(Use a punch bowl.)

1 bottle of moselle;
½ pint of sherry;
2 tablespoonfuls of sugar;
1 lemon;
1 sprig of verbena;

Peel the lemon very thinly, using only sufficient of the peel to produce the desired flavor; add the other ingredients; strain and ice.

ENGLISH CURAÇOA.
(Use a punch bowl.)

6 ounces of very thin orange peel;
1 pint of whiskey;
1 pint of clarified syrup;
1 drachm powdered alum;
1 drachm carbonate of potash;

Place the orange peel in a bottle, which will hold a quart with the whiskey; cork tightly, and put it aside for 10 to 12 days, shaking it frequently. Then strain out the peel, add the syrup; shake well, and let it stand for 3 days. Take out a teacupful into a mortar, and beat up with alum and potash; when well mixed, pour it back into the bottle, and let it remain thus for a week.

The curacoa will then be perfectly clear and equal in flavor to the best imported article.

DUKE OF NORFOLK PUNCH FOR BOTTLING.

20 quarts of French brandy (Martell);
30 lemons;
30 oranges;
30 quarts of cold, boiled water;
15 pounds of double-refined sugar;
6 quarts of new milk;

Pare off the peel of the oranges and lemons very thinly, excluding all the white rind; infuse in the brandy for 12 hours; dissolve the sugar in the water; add the juice of the oranges and of 24 of the lemons; pour this upon the brandy and peels, mixing it thoroughly; strain through a very fine hair sieve into a barrel that has held spirits, and add the milk.

Stir and bung close, after it has been six weeks in a warm cellar, pour it into perfectly clean and dry bottles, and cork well. This will keep for years and improve with age.

BISHOP À LA PRUSSE.
(Use a punch bowl for mixing.)

1 bottle of claret;
½ pound of pounded loaf sugar;
4 good-sized bitter oranges;

Roast the oranges until they are of a pale-brown color; lay them in a tureen, and cover them with the sugar, adding 3 glasses of claret; cover the tureen, and let it stand until the next day.

When required for use, place the tureen in a pan of boiling water, press the oranges with a spoon, and run the juice through a sieve. Boil the remainder of the claret; add the strained juice, and serve warm in glasses. Port wine may be substituted for claret, and lemons may be used instead of oranges, but this is not often done when claret is used.

COLD RUBY PUNCH.
(Use a punch bowl.)

1 quart of Batavia arrac;
1 quart of port wine;
3 pints of green tea;
1 pound of loaf sugar;
Juice of 6 lemons;
½ pineapple, cut in small slices;

Dissolve the sugar in the tea, and add other materials served iced.

ROCHESTER PUNCH.
(For a small party.)

2 bottles of sparkling Catawba;
2 bottles of sparkling Isabella;
1 bottle of Sauterne;
2 wine glasses of maraschino;
2 wine glasses of curaçoa;

Flavor with ripe strawberries; should strawberries not be in season, add a few drops of extract of peach or vanilla. Ice in a cooler, place pieces of different fruits in season into a fancy wine glass, and serve.

FEDORA.
(Use a large bar glass.)

1 pony of brandy (Martell);
1 pony of curaçoa;
½ pony of Jamaica rum;
½ pony of Bourbon;

1 tablespoonful of powdered sugar, dissolve in a little water;
1 slice of lemon;
Fill the tumbler with fine ice; shake well, and ornament with berries or small pieces of orange; serve with a straw.

ORANGE PUNCH.
(Use a bowl for mixing.)

¾ pint of rum;
¾ pint of brandy (Martell,;
½ pint of porter;
3½ pints of boiling water;
¾ pound of loaf sugar;
4 oranges;

Infuse the peel of 2, and the juice of 4 oranges with the sugar in the water for half an hour; strain and add the porter, rum, and brandy. Sugar may be added, if it is desired sweeter.

A liquor glass of curaçoa, noyeau, or, maraschino is considered an improvement.

Instead of using both, rum and brandy, 1½ pint of either alone will answer.

This is also an excellent receipt for lemon punch by substituting lemons for oranges.

CURRANT SHRUB.
(Use a bowl for mixing; general rule for preparing.)

1 quart of strained currant juice;
1½ pound of loaf sugar;

Boil it gently for 8 or 10 minutes, skimming it well; take it off, and, when lukewarm, add ¼ gill of brandy to every pint of shrub. Bottle tight.

A little shrub mixed with ice water makes a delicious drink. Shrub may be made of cherry or raspberry juice by this method, but the quantity of sugar must be reduced.

PLATE No. 15.

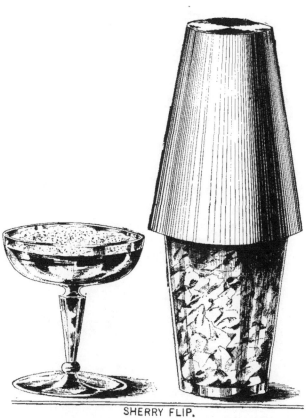

SHERRY FLIP.

Copyrighted, 1888.

WHITE PLUSH.
(Use a small bar glass.)

Hand the bottle of Bourbon or rye whiskey to the customer, and let him help himself. Fill up the glass with fresh milk. This is what is called "White Plush," it has been an old-time drink known for many years.

HOT BRANDY SLING.
(Use a hot water glass.)

1 lump of sugar, dissolve well with a little hot water;
1 wine glass of brandy (Martell);
Fill up with hot water, stir up with a spoon, grate a little nutmeg on top, and serve.

If the customer desires it, cut a slice of lemon into this drink.

PORT WINE SANGAREE.
(Use a small bar glass.)

1 teaspoonful of sugar, dissolve well with a little water;
1 or 2 lumps of ice;
1 wine glass of port wine;
Stir up with a spoon, remove the piece of ice if required; grate a little nutmeg on top, and serve.

COLD WHISKEY SLING.
(Use a small bar glass.)

1 teaspoonful of sugar;
$\frac{1}{2}$ wine glass of water, dissolve well;
1 or 2 small lumps of ice;
1 wine glass of whiskey;
Mix well, grate a little nutmeg on top, and serve.
This is an old-fashioned drink, generally called for by old gentlemen.

PORT WINE COBBLER.
(Use a large bar glass.)

½ tablespoonful of sugar;
1 pony glass of orchard syrup;
½ wine glass of water, dissolve well with a spoon;
Fill the glass with fine ice;
1½ wineglassful of port wine;
Mix up well, and ornament with grapes, berries, etc., if in season, in a tasteful manner, and serve.

ROCK AND RYE.
(Use a whiskey glass.)

This drink must be very carefully prepared, and care must also be taken to procure the best rock candy syrup as well as the best rye whiskey, this drink being an effective remedy for sore throats, etc.

In serving rock and rye, put ½ tablespoonful of rock candy syrup into the glass, place a spoon in it, and hand the bottle of rye whiskey to the customer, to help himself; a few drops of lemon juice adds to the flavor of this drink, helps to heal sore throats, and makes it more palatable.

GIN SOUR.
(Use a large bar glass.)

½ tablespoonful of sugar;
2 or 3 dashes of lemon juice;
1 dash of lime juice;
1 squirt of syphon selters water;
Dissolve the sugar and lemon well with a spoon;
¾ of a wine glass filled with finely shaved ice;
1 wine glass of Holland gin;
Mix well, strain it into a sour glass, dress with a little fruit in season, and serve.

PEACH AND HONEY.
(Use a small bar glass.)

1 tablespoonful of honey;
1 wine glass of peach brandy;
Stir well with a spoon, and serve.

This drink is a great favorite in winter, and was formerly called for as often as rock and rye is now.

ST. CROIX SOUR.
(Use a large bar glass.)

$\frac{1}{2}$ tablespoonful of sugar;
3 or 4 dashes of lemon juice;
1 squirt of syphon selters water, dissolve well with a spoon;
$\frac{3}{4}$ glass finely shaved ice;
1 wine glass St. Croix rum;

Mix well, place your seasonable fruit in a sour glass, and strain the above ingredients into the fruit, and serve.

COFFEE COCKTAIL.
(Use a large bar glass.)

$\frac{1}{4}$ tablespoonful of sugar;
1 yolk of an egg;
$\frac{3}{4}$ wine glass of port wine;
$\frac{1}{4}$ wine glass of brandy (Martell);

Fill a glass with finely shaved ice; shake up well; strain into a cocktail glass, putting in a medium-sized olive, and serve.

GIN RICKEY.
(Use a medium size fizz glass.)

1 or 2 pieces of ice;
Squeeze the juice of 1 good-sized lime or 2 small ones;
1 wine glass of Tom or Holland gin if required;

Fill up the glass with club soda, carbonic or selters if required, and serve with a spoon.

TRILBY COCKTAIL.
(Use a large bar glass.)

Fill up with shaved ice;
2 dashes of absinthe;
2 or 3 dashes of orange bitters;
2 or 3 dashes of "Parafait d'Amour;"
½ wine glass of Scotch whiskey;
½ wine glass of Italian vermouth;

Stir up well with a spoon; strain into a cocktail glass, putting in cherries, and squeeze a piece of lemon peel on top, then serve.

MORNING COCKTAIL.
(Use a large bar glass.)

Fill up a glass with finely shaved ice;
2 dashes of curaçoa;
2 dashes of maraschino;
2 dashes of absinthe;
3 or 4 dashes of bitters (Boker's genuine only);
½ wine glass of brandy;
½ wine glass of vermouth;

Stir up well with a spoon; strain into a cocktail glass, putting in a cherry; twist a piece of lemon peel on top, and serve.

OLD FASHIONED WHISKEY COCKTAIL.

Take a whiskey tumbler, and put into it:
¼ of a teaspoonful of sugar;
2 small lumps of ice;
2 or 3 dashes of bitters (Boker's genuine only);
1 or 2 dashes of curaçoa or absinthe if required;
1 wine glass of whiskey;

Stir up well with a spoon until the ingredients are well mixed, squeeze a piece of lemon peel on top, and serve, in the same glass.

IRISH COCKTAIL.
(Use a large bar glass.)

Fill up a glass with shaved ice;
2 or 3 dashes of absinthe;
1 dash of maraschino;
1 dash of curaçoa;
2 dashes of bitters (Boker's genuine only);
1 wineglassful of Irish whiskey;
Stir up well with a spoon, strain into a cocktail glass, putting in a medium-sized olive, then squeeze a piece of lemon peel on top, and serve.

CINCINNATI COCKTAIL.
(Use a large bar glass.)

½ glassful of lager beer;
½ glassful of soda or ginger ale if required;
This is a very cooling drink, and is drank very much by the people of Cincinnati, during the warm weather.

CHOCOLATE COCKTAIL.
(Use a large bar glass.)

1 yolk of an egg;
½ wineglassful of chartreuse;
½ wineglassful of port wine;
¼ teaspoonful of ground chocolate (sweet);
Fill up a glass with finely shaved ice, shake well with a shaker, strain it into a cocktail glass, and serve.

PUNCH À LA DWYER.
(Use a punch bowl for mixing.)

12 lumps of cut loaf sugar;
1 lemon, cut in slices;
½ pineapple, cut in slices;
1 orange, cut in slices;
4 quarts of club soda or imported German selters water;

2 wine glasses of cognac (Martell);
1 quart of Burgundy;
1 quart of champagne (Piper Heidsieck);
Stir up well with a ladle;
Place the bowl into a large dish, filled with ice; serve in fancy wine glasses, and this will make a very satisfactory punch. If in season, place a few strawberries into every glass.

PHILIPPINE PUNCH.
(Use a large bar glass.)

¼ tablespoonful of sugar;
3 or 4 dashes of lemon or lime juice;
1 wine glass of Jamaica rum;
2 or 3 small lumps of ice;
Fill up a glass with club soda, stir up slowly with a spoon, and serve.
This will make a very refreshing drink for soldiers.

OLD STYLE AMERICAN PUNCH.
(Use a large bar glass.)

½ tablespoonful of sugar;
3 or 4 dashes of fresh lime juice;
1 wine glass of old American whiskey;
3 or 4 lumps of broken ice;
Fill a goblet up with domestic ginger ale, stir well with a spoon, decorate with fruit in season, in a tasteful manner, and serve with a straw.

BRANDY AND MINT.
(Use a small bar glass.)

1 lump cut loaf sugar, dissolved with spoon in water;
1 sprig of mint, slightly bruised;
2 lumps of ice;
1 wine glass of brandy (Martell);
Serve with spoon, and water on side.

ABSINTHE FRAPPE.
(Use a large bar glass.)

1 wine glass of absinthe;
2 or 3 dashes of anisette;
Fill glass with finely shaved ice;
Shake up long enough, until the outside of the shaker is thoroughly covered with ice; strain into fancy bar glass; fill up glass with ice-cold syphon vichy water and serve.

CHAMPAGNE CUP.
(Use a punch bowl for mixing.)

½ pineapple, cut in slices;
3 or 4 slices of cucumber (rind or peel only);
1 box strawberries (thoroughly cleaned);
1 pony glass of curaçoa;
1 or 2 bottles of club soda (according to the size of the party);
1 quart of champagne (Piper Heidsieck);
Stir up slowly with a ladle, place the bowl into a large dish filled with ice, pour into fancy wine glasses, and place the fruits in season into the wine glasses, then serve.

CLARET FLIP.
(Use a large bar glass.)

1 fresh egg;
½ tablespoonful of sugar;
½ glassful of shaved ice;
1½ wineglassful of claret wine;
Shake it well until it is thoroughly mixed; strain it into a fancy bar glass, grate a little nutmeg on top, and serve.

This is a very delicious drink, and gives strength to delicate people.

TEA PUNCH FOR THE WINTER.
(Use a punch bowl.)

½ pint of good brandy (Martell);
½ pint of rum;
¼ pound of loaf sugar, dissolved in water with a ladle;
1 ounce of best green tea;
1 quart of boiling water;
1 large lemon;

Infuse the tea in the water; warm a silver or other metal bowl until quite hot; place into it the brandy, rum, sugar, and juice of the lemon.

The oil of the lemon peel should be first obtained by rubbing with a few lumps of the sugar.

Set the contents of the bowl on fire; and while flaming, pour in the tea gradually, stirring with a ladle. It will continue to burn for some time, and should be ladled into glasses while in that condition. A heated metal bowl will cause the punch to burn longer than if a china bowl is used.

This drink can be made to taste very palatable.

DUKE OF NORFOLK PUNCH.
(For a small party.)

3 quarts of brandy (Martell);
1 quart of sherry wine;
2 quarts of milk;
2 pounds of sugar;
1 lemon;
2 oranges;

Pare off the peel of the oranges and lemons very thinly; put the peel and all the juice into a vessel with a close-fitting lid. Pour on the brandy, wine, and milk, then add the sugar, after having dissolved it in sufficient water.

Mix well, and cover close for 24 hours; strain until clear, and it is ready for serving.

PUNCH À LA ROMAINE.
(Party of twelve.)

¾ quart of Jamaica rum;
¾ quart of sherry wine;
5 lemons;
2 oranges, cut in slices;
5 eggs;

Dissolve the sugar in the juice of the lemons and oranges, adding the thin rind of one orange; strain through a sieve into a bowl, and add, by degrees, the whites of the eggs beaten to a froth; place the bowl on ice for a while; then stir in briskly the rum and sherry wine, and serve.

BRANDY SPLIT.
(Use a medium size fizz glass.)

1 pony glass of brandy (Martell);
1 or 2 small lumps of ice;
1 bottle of club soda;

Fill up the glass, and serve. As a rule, this drink is generally drank by a party of two; 1 bottle of soda is sufficient to fill both glasses, and, therefore, is called a split.

WEDDING PUNCH FOR A PARTY.
(Use a large punch bowl.)

¼ pint of pineapple syrup;
½ pint of lemon juice;
1 wine glass of lemon syrup;
½ pound of loaf sugar;
1 quart of boiling water or imported German selters water;
1 quart of claret or port wine;
3 grains of vanilla;
1 grain of ambergris;
1 pint of strong brandy (Martell);

Rub the vanilla and ambergris with the sugar into

the brandy thoroughly; let it stand in a corked bottle for a few hours, shaking it occasionally.

Then add the lemon juice, pineapple juice and wine; filter through a flannel, and finally add the syrup.

In dishing out, fill the glasses full of punch, place the different fruits in season into it, and serve.

PORTER CUP FOR A PARTY.
(Use a fancy glass pitcher.)

1 bottle of porter;
1 bottle of Bass' ale;
1 pony glass of brandy (Martell);
½ tablespoonful of syrup of ginger;
5 or 6 small lumps of crystal ice;
1 teaspoonful of carbonated soda;

Stir up well, and grate a little nutmeg on top.

Mix the porter and ale in a covered jug; add the brandy, syrup of ginger, and nutmeg; cover it, then expose it to the cold for half an hour.

When serving, put in the carbonate of soda.

SHERRY COCKTAIL.
(Use a large bar glass.)

¾ glassful of shaved ice;
2 or 3 dashes of bitters (Boker's genuine only);
1 dash of maraschino;
1 wine glass of sherry wine;

Stir up well with a spoon; strain into a cocktail glass, put a cherry into it, squeeze a piece of lemon peel on top, and serve.

CHAMPAGNE PUNCH.
(Use a punch bowl for mixing.)

3 or 4 lumps of loaf sugar;
1 orange, cut in slices;
5 or 6 drops of lemon juice;

5 or 6 slices of pineapple;
½ wine glass of curaçoa;
1 quart of champagne (Piper Heidsieck);
1 bottle of club soda;
Stir up with a ladle; put bowl into a vessel filled with ice, in order to cool it; fill the ingredients into fancy champagne glasses, and serve.

This will make a very tasteful beverage for a small party.

EGG SOUR.
(Use a large bar glass.)

1 tablespoonful of powdered sugar;
2 dashes of lemon juice;
1 pony glass of curaçoa;
1 pony glass of brandy (Martell);
1 yolk of an egg;
¾ glass of finely shaved ice;
Shake up well with a shaker; strain into a medium-sized fancy wine glass, and serve.

PARISIAN POUSSE CAFÉ.
(Use a sherry wine glass.)

$1/_3$ wineglassful of chartreuse (green);
$1/_3$ wineglassful of curaçoa (red);
$1/_3$ wineglassful of Kirschwasser;
Top it off with a little French cognac, and serve. Care should be taken in placing in the different cordials, in order to have each color separated and not running together.

HOT EGG NOGG.
(Use a large bar glass.)

Mix as follows:
1 fresh egg;
½ tablespoonful of powdered sugar;
½ wineglassful of cognac (Martell);

½ wineglassful of Jamaica rum;
Fill up a goblet with boiling hot milk, grate a little nutmeg on top, and serve. It is to be understood that this drink must be stirred and not shaken up.

HOT BRANDY PUNCH.
(Use a hot water glass.)

1 or 2 lumps of loaf sugar;
2 or 3 drops of lemon juice;
Dissolve with a little hot water, before putting in brandy;
1 wine glass of brandy (Martell);
Fill up balance with hot water, put a slice of lemon into it, stir up well with a spoon, grate a little nutmeg on top, and serve.

HOT SCOTCH WHISKEY PUNCH.
(Use a hot water glass.)

1 or 2 lumps of loaf sugar;
Dissolve well with a little hot water;
1 wineglassful of Scotch whiskey;
Fill up a glass with hot water, stir up well with a spoon, put a slice of lemon into it, grate a little nutmeg on top, and serve.

BRANDY SMASH.
(Use a large bar glass.)

¼ tablespoonful of powdered sugar;
1 squirt of syphon selters or vichy;
3 or 4 sprigs of fresh mint, dissolve well with spoon until the essence of the mint is extracted;
1 wineglassful of brandy (Martell);
Fill up the glass with finely shaved ice, stir up well with a spoon, strain into a sour or fancy wine glass.
Put a slice of pineapple, oranges, lemon, and a few strawberries into a glass, and serve.

HIGHBALL.
(Use a medium size fizz glass.)
Mix as follows:
2 or 3 lumps of clear crystal ice;
1 wine glass of Scotch whiskey;

Fill up a glass with ice-cold syphon vichy; if customer requires whiskey, gin, brandy or highball, you must then use the liquor accordingly.

COFFEE COBBLER.
(Use a large bar glass.)
Fill the glass nearly up with finely broken ice;
1 tablespoonful of fine sugar;
1 pony glass of cognac (Martell);

Fill up the glass with good, strong, black coffee; stir up well with spoon, and serve with a straw.

TEA COBBLER.
(Use a large bar glass.)
Fill the glass nearly up with finely broken ice;
1 tablespoonful of fine sugar;
1 pony glass of Jamaica rum;

Fill up the glass with good, strong, black tea; stir up well with a spoon, and serve with a straw.

BRANDY JULEP.
(Use a large bar glass.
$\frac{3}{4}$ tablespoonful of sugar;
$\frac{1}{2}$ wineglassful of water or selters;
3 or 4 sprigs of fresh mint, dissolve well until all the essence of the mint is extracted;

Fill up the glass with finely shaved ice;
1 wineglassful of brandy (Martell);

Stir up well with a spoon; ornament this drink with mint, oranges, pineapple, and berries, in a tasty manner; sprinkle a little sugar on top of it; dash with Jamaica rum, and serve.

CHAMPAGNE FRAPPE.

In order to have the wine frapped, it is proper to have a special ice box made for this purpose where champagne freezes in the natural temperature of the ice box, which, as a rule, is built to answer that purpose; but in case you have not a champagne freezer or ice box, take a large-sized pail, fill it with ice as finely shaved as possible, throw a few handfuls of rock salt into it, then twist and twirl bottles right and left, until your wine becomes cold, stiff, and frozen. If you do not happen to succeed in frapping it quickly enough, it is advisable to loosen the cork, taking it out, then placing a clean napkin tight over the neck of the bottle.

This must not be done until the wine gets into a very cold state, otherwise the wine will squirt and foam out of the bottle.

Then twist it forward and backward as fast as possible, and you will soon have the wine in proper condition and frapped.

It is, furthermore, advisable to have the champagne glasses, which are to be used, filled and chilled with finely shaved ice, and when the wine is ready to serve, empty the ice out of the glasses, and fill up with wine and serve.

Piper Heidsieck is the proper wine to use for frapping.

HOT ENGLISH RUM PUNCH.
(Use a punch bowl.)

Mix as follows:
1 quart of ale;
1 gill of old English rum;

PLATE No. 16.

ST. CHARLES PUNCH.   BRANDY PUNCH.

Copyrighted, 1888.

4 fresh raw eggs;
4 ounces of powdered sugar;

Heat the ale in a saucepan; beat up the eggs and sugar; add the nutmeg and rum, and put it all into a pitcher.

When the ale is near to a boil, put it into another pitcher; pour it very gradually into the pitcher containing the eggs, etc., stirring all the while briskly to prevent the eggs from curdling.

Then pour the contents of the two pitchers from one into the other until the mixture is as smooth as cream, and serve in a punch bowl.

CREME DE MENTHE.
(Use a cocktail glass.)

Have the cocktail glass packed up with finely shaved ice;

Fill up the glass with creme de Menthe and serve.

In case you are asked for a creme de Menthe frappé, you must put the above ingredients in a shaker, fill up the shaker with ice, shake well until the outside of the shaker is covered with ice, strain into a fancy glass and serve.

WHISKEY SMASH.
(Use a large bar glass.)

½ tablespoonful of sugar;
½ wineglass of water or selters;
3 or 4 sprigs of fresh mint, dissolved well until all the essence of the mint is extracted;
½ glass of shaved ice;
1 wineglass of whiskey;

Stir up well with a spoon, strain into a fancy bar glass, and ornament with a little fruit in season, and serve.

GIN DAISY.
(Use a large bar glass.)

½ tablespoonful of sugar;
2 or 3 dashes of lemon juice;
1 dash of lime juice;
1 squirt of syphon vichy or selters, dissolve with the lemon and lime juice;
¾ of the glass filled with fine-shaved ice;
1 wine glass of good gin;
Fill the glass with shaved ice;
½ pony glass of chartreuse (yellow);
Stir up well with a spoon, then take a fancy glass, have it dressed with fruit in season in a tasty manner, and strain the mixture into it and serve.

This drink is very palatable and will taste good to most anybody.

REMSEN COOLER.
(Use a medium size fizz glass.)

Peel a lemon as you would an apple;
Place the rind or peeling into the fizz glass;
2 or 3 lumps of crystal ice;
1 wine glass of Remsen Scotch whiskey;
Fill up the balance with club soda;
Stir up slowly with a spoon and serve.

In this country it is often the case that people call a Remsen cooler where they want Old Tom gin or Sloe gin, instead of Scotch whiskey; it is therefore the bartender's duty to mix as desired.

APPLE JACK COCKTAIL.
(Use a large size bar glass.)

¾ glass of fine-shaved ice;
2 or 3 dashes of gum syrup, very careful not using too much;

1½ or 2 dashes of bitters (Boker's genuine only);
1 or 2 dashes of curaçoa;
1 wine glass of apple jack;
Stir up well with a spoon and strain it into a cocktail glass. Put in a cherry or medium-size olive; squeeze a piece of lemon peel on top and serve.

This is a popular and a palatable drink.

SNOW BALL.
(Use a bar glass.)

Fill glass full of fine-shaved ice;
½ tablespoonful of sugar;
1 wine glass whiskey;
White of an egg;
Place ingredients into shaker, and fill with ice; shake well and strain into large size fizz glass and fill with imported ginger ale.

BIJOU COCKTAIL.
(Use a large bar glass.)

¾ glass filled with fine shaved ice;
$1/3$ wine glass chartreuse (green);
$1/3$ wine glass vermouth (Italian);
$1/3$ wine glass of Plymouth gin;
1 dash of orange bitters.
Mix well with a spoon, strain into a cocktail glass; add a cherry or medium-size olive, squeeze a piece of lemon peel on top and serve.

COL. BROWN PUNCH.

Mix some lemonade, strain into a pitcher, half fill the glasses with small lumps of ice, putting in ½ pony glass of French cognac into each glass and a few slices of fruit, as pineapple, oranges, or berries, etc., and fill the glasses with the lemonade mixture.

PORT WINE LEMONADE.
(Use a large bar glass.)

¾ tablespoonful of sugar;
6 to 8 dashes of lemon juice;
Fill tumbler nearly full with fine-shaved ice; fill the balance of tumbler up with water; shake up well with a shaker.

Ornament with fruit in season and top it off with 1 wine glass of port wine.

Be careful to have port wine flowing on top of lemonade, and serve with a straw.

VIRGIN STRAWBERRY ICE CREAM.
(Use a punch bowl.)

3 pints of sweet cream;
1 pint of milk to each quart of strawberries;
2 pounds of powdered sugar;
Dissolve the sugar;
Strain through a very fine sieve and serve.
This makes a very nice refreshment for ladies.

TURKISH SHERBET.
(Use a punch bowl.)

Mix as follows:
2 quarts of sweet wine;
2 quarts of water;
4 pounds of sugar;
4 lemons, juice only;
6 oranges, juice only;
1 pound blanched almonds;
1 pound muscatel grapes;
½ pound figs, cut up;
½ pound seedless raisins;
$1^{1}/_{3}$ dozen eggs, whites only;
1 dozen cloves, a small piece of cinnamon and a little caramel coloring.

Make a hot syrup of the sugar and water and pour it over the raisins, cloves and cinnamon.

When cool, add orange and lemon juice and wine. Strain and freeze in the usual manner.

Take out the spices and add the scalded raisins, figs, grapes and almonds last.

SARATOGA COOLER.
(Use a large bar glass.)

3 or 4 lumps of crystal ice;
1 teaspoonful of powdered sugar;
3 or 4 dashes of lime or lemon juice;
1 bottle of ginger ale;
Stir up well with a spoon and serve.

HORSE'S NECK.
(Use a large size fizz glass.)

Peel a lemon in one long string, place in glass, so that one end hangs over the head of glass;
2 or 3 dashes of bitters (Boker's genuine only);
1 wine glass whiskey, rye, Scotch, or Irish, as requested;
3 or 4 lumps of broken ice;
Fill up with syphon vichy, or ginger ale, if required.

EYE OPENER.
(Use a large bar glass.)

$\frac{3}{4}$ glass full of fine-shaved ice;
1 egg, the white only;
$\frac{3}{4}$ wine glass of absinthe;
$\frac{1}{4}$ wine glass of whiskey, if required, Tom gin or Scotch whiskey; shake well with a shaker;
Strain into a medium-size fizz glass, fill up with cold carbonic water, put a little fruit in the glass and serve.

APOLLINARIS LEMONADE.
(Use a large bar glass.)

7 to 8 dashes of lemon juice;
¾ tablespoonful of powdered sugar;
3 or 4 lumps of broken ice;

Fill up glass with apollinaris water, strain into fizz glass, and serve with straw.

No fruit should be used in making this drink.

CLARET LEMONADE.
(Use a large bar glass.)

¾ tablespoonful of sugar;
6 to 8 dashes of lemon juice;

Fill tumbler nearly full with fine-shaved ice, and the balance with water; shake up well with a shaker, ornament with fruits in season and top it off with

½ glass of claret wine; be careful to have the claret flowing on top of lemonade, and serve with a straw.

MARASCHINO PUNCH.
(Use a large punch bowl.)

Mix as follows:
4 pounds of sugar;
2 quarts of water;
4 lemons, the juice only;
4 oranges, the juice only;
1 quart of maraschino;
1 dozen eggs, the whites only, whipped;

Mix the sugar, water and juice of punch together; strain, freeze, add the whipped whites of the eggs, and beat up and serve.

RUSSIAN PUNCH.
(Use a large punch bowl.)

Mix as follows:
2 quarts of black tea made as for drinking;
1 quart of water;
1 quart of port wine;
1 pint of brandy (Martell);
3 pounds of sugar;
½ dozen lemons;
Little caramel to color;

Cut the lemons in small slices in a bowl, make a boiling syrup of the sugar and water; pour over and let stand till cold. Add tea, liquor, strain and then freeze.

Keep slices of lemon on ice and mix in when frozen, and serve.

THORN COCKTAIL.
(Use a large size bar glass.)

Fill glass ¾ full of fine-shaved ice;
1 dash of orange bitters;
½ wineglass of calisaya;
¼ wine glass of old Tom gin;
¼ wine glass of French vermouth;

Stir well with a spoon, strain into a cocktail glass, putting in a cherry, squeeze a piece of lemon peel on top and serve.

MONTANA COCKTAIL.
(Use a large bar glass.)

¾ glass full of fine-shaved ice;
2 or 3 dashes of anisette;
2 or 3 dashes of bitters (Boker's genuine only);
½ wine glass of French vermouth;
¼ wine glass of Sloe gin;

Stir up well with a spoon, strain into a cocktail glass; squeeze a piece of lemon peel on top and serve.

STAR COCKTAIL.
(Use a large size bar glass.)

Fill glass ¾ full of fine-shaved ice;
1 or 2 dashes of gum;
1 dash of curaçoa;
3 dashes of bitters (Boker's genuine only);
½ wine glass of French vermouth;
½ wine glass of apple jack;
Stir well with a spoon, strain into a cocktail glass, squeeze a piece of lemon peel on top and serve.

SILVER COCKTAIL.
(Use a large bar glass.)

1 or 2 dashes of gum;
2 or 3 dashes of orange bitters;
3 dashes of maraschino;
½ wine glass of French vermouth;
½ wine glass of gin;
Stir up well with a spoon, strain into a cocktail glass; squeeze a piece of lemon peel on top and serve.

OYSTER COCKTAIL.
(Use a medium size wine glass.)

5 to 6 squirts of ketchup, enough to fill the bottom of the glass;
1 or 2 medium-size oysters;
Sufficient pepper and salt to season it well;
1 small dash of lemon juice, and serve.

In restaurants larger glasses are used, more oysters and the ingredients in proportion;

ST. JOSEPH COCKTAIL.
(Use a large bar glass.)

¾ glass of fine-shaved ice;
1 or 2 dashes of gum syrup;
2 or 3 dashes of bitters (Boker's genuine only);

½ wine glass of French vermouth;
½ wine glass of Scotch whiskey.;
Stir up well with a spoon, strain into a cocktail glass; putting a medium-size olive into it, squeeze a piece of lemon peel on top and serve.

LITTLE EGYPT.
(Use a large bar glass.)

¾ glass full of fine-shaved ice;
2 or 3 dashes of bitters (Boker's genuine only);
2 or 3 dashes of absinthe;
2 or 3 dashes of vermouth;
1 wine glass of sherry;
Stir up well with a spoon, strain into a medium-size wine glass and serve.

MARGUERITE COCKTAIL.
(Use a large bar glass.)

Fill glass ¾ full of fine-shaved ice;
2 or 3 dashes of orange bitters;
2 or 3 dashes of anisette;
½ wine glass of French vermouth;
½ wine glass of Plymouth gin;
Stir up well with a spoon, strain into a cocktail glass, putting in a cherry, squeeze a piece of lemon peel on top and serve.

IMPERIAL COCKTAIL.
(Use a large bar glass.)

¾ glass full of fine-shaved ice;
1 or 2 dashes of orange bitters;
1 or 2 dashes of absinthe;
½ wine glass of French vermouth;
½ wine glass of maraschino;

Stir up well with a spoon, strain into a cocktail glass, putting in a cherry, squeeze a piece of lemon peel on top and serve.

MAIDEN'S DREAM.

¾ pony glass of benedictine, or creme de cocoa;
Fill up the pony glass with fine cream, and serve.
This is a very palatable drink and is admired much by ladies.

REFORM COCKTAIL.
(Use a large bar glass.)

¾ full of fine-shaved ice;
2 or 3 dashes of bitters (Boker's genuine only);
½ wine glass of French vermouth;
½ wine glass of sherry;

Stir up well with a spoon, strain into a cocktail glass, putting a cherry into it, squeeze a piece of lemon peel on top and serve.

KLONDYKE COCKTAIL.
(Use a large bar glass.)

¾ glass full of fine-shaved ice;
3 or 4 dashes of bitters (Boker's genuine only);
½ wine glass of applejack;
½ wine glass of French vermouth;

Stir up well with a spoon, strain into a cocktail glass, putting in a medium-size olive, squeeze a piece of lemon peel on top and serve.

GOLDEN THISTLE.
(Use a large bar glass.)

½ medium-size spoon of sugar;
3 or 4 dashes of lemon juice;
1 yolk of a fresh egg;

1 wine glass of Scotch whiskey;

Shake up well with a shaker, strain into a medium-size fizz glass, fill the glass with syphon vichy and serve.

This drink must be drank as soon as mixed, otherwise it will lose its flavor.

MORNING DAISY.
(Use a large bar glass.)

¾ glass of fine-shaved ice;
3 or 4 dashes of lemon juice;
¼ tablespoonful of sugar;
3 or 4 dashes of absinthe;
1 white of an egg;
1 wine glass of Scotch whiskey;

Shake up well with shaker, strain into a medium-size wine glass and serve.

OLIVETTE COCKTAIL.
(Use a large bar glass.)

¾ glass of fine-shaved ice;
1 or 2 dashes of gum;
3 or 4 dashes of orange bitters;
3 or 4 dashes of absinthe;
1 wine glass of Plymouth gin;

Stir up well with a spoon, strain into cocktail glass, putting in an olive, squeeze a piece of lemon peel on top and serve.

TENDERLOIN REVIVER.

Peel off the rind of a good-size lemon, the same as you would an apple, place the peel into a large bar glass, as a Tom Collins' glass;

1 wine glass of Scotch whiskey;
2 or 3 lumps of fine crystal ice;
Fill glass with imported ginger ale, stir with a spoon slowly and serve.

BRAZIL COCKTAIL.
(Use a large bar glass.)

¾ glass of fine-shaved ice;
3 or 4 dashes of bitters (Boker's genuine only);
3 or 4 dashes of absinthe;
½ wine glass of French vermouth;
½ wine glass of sherry wine;
Stir up well with a spoon, strain into a cocktail glass, putting in a cherry, squeeze a piece of lemon peel on top and serve.

BLACK THORN.
(Use a large bar glass.)

3 or 4 dashes of absinthe;
3 or 4 dashes of bitters (Boker's genuine only);
½ wine glass of French vermouth;
½ wine glass of Irish whiskey;
Stir up well with a spoon, strain into a medium-sized wine glass and serve.

BRADFORD À LA MARTINI.
(Use a large bar glass.)

¾ glass of fine-shaved ice;
3 or 4 dashes of orange bitters;
The peel of one lemon into mixing glass;
½ wine glass of Tom gin;
½ wine glass of vermouth;
Shake well with a shaker, strain into a cocktail glass, put a medium-sized olive into it and serve.

APRIL SHOWER.
(Use a small size fizz glass.)
1 pony glass of brandy (Martell);
½ pony glass of benedictine;
Juice of ½ orange;

Take the top part of an absinthe glass, fill it with fine-shaved ice, and squirt syphon seltser through ice, enough to fill glass holding your brandy and benedictine.

TUXEDO COCKTAIL.
(Use a large bar glass.)
¾ glass full of fine-shaved ice;
1 or 2 dashes of maraschino;
1 dash of absinthe;
2 or 3 dashes of orange bitters;
½ wine glass of French vermouth;
½ wine glass Sir Burnett's Tom gin;

Stir up well with a spoon, strain into a cocktail glass, putting in cherry, squeeze a piece of lemon peel on top and serve.

AMERICAN GLORY.
(Use a large fancy champagne goblet.)
Squeeze the juice of ½ fine orange;
¼ glass full of champagne (Piper Heidsieck);
2 or 3 pieces of crystal ice;

Fill glass up with apollinaris water, stir up gently with a spoon and serve. This is an excellent drink before going to bed, after having been out late to a party.

HIGH LIFE.

(Use a large bar glass.)

1 or 2 dashes of lemon juice;
2 or 3 pieces of crystal ice;
1 pony glass of brandy (Martell);
¼ spoonful of sugar, fill up glass with club soda and serve.

WIDOW'S KISS.

(Use a medium size wine glass.)

1 yolk of a fresh egg;
$1/3$ glass of maraschino;
$1/3$ glass of green chartreuse;
$1/3$ glass of benedictine, and serve.

TURF COCKTAIL.

(Use a large bar glass.)

¾ full of fine shaved ice;
2 or 3 dashes of orange bitters;
2 or 3 dashes of maraschino;
2 dashes of absinthe;
½ wine glass of French vermouth;
½ wine glass of Plymouth gin;

Stir up well with a spoon, strain into a cocktail glass, putting in a medium size olive; and serve.

WINES WITH A FORMAL DINNER

Before Meals or With Soup

SHERRY:
Usual names—Amontillado and other dry types. See also under desserts. Alcohol 19% to 21%. Serve at room temperature.

FISH COURSE

CHAMPAGNE (LIGHT GOLDEN):
Extra dry—dry, brut—very dry. Delicate light taste. Alcohol 13% to 14%. Serve thoroughly chilled. See also under desserts.

CHIANTI (WHITE):
Alcohol 12% to 13%. Serve at room temperature.

RHINE (WHITE WINE):
Usual names—Barr Traminer, Moselle, Riesling, Sylvaner. Dry and light. Alcohol 10%. Serve thoroughly chilled. May be served in pale green glass.

SPARKLING WINES:
Usual names—Sparkling Chablis, Sparkling Moselle. Similar to dry champagne. Alcohol 12% to 14%. Serve thoroughly chilled. See also under roast.

WHITE BORDEAUX:
Usual names—Barsacs, Graves. Some semi-sweet but usually dry. Alcohol 10% to 12%. Serve 20° below room temperature. See also under desserts.

WHITE BURGUNDY:
Usual names—Chablis, Meursault, Pouilly-Fuisse. Extremely dry. Alcohol 12% to 15%. Serve 20° below room temperature.

ENTREE

CHIANTI (RED):
From dry to slightly sweet. Alcohol 12% to 13%. Serve at room temperature.

ROAST

RED BURGUNDIES:
Usual names—Beaune, Chambertin, Macon, Nuits St. Georges, Pommard, Richebourg, Volnay. Rich flavor and heavy body. Alcohol 12% to 15%.

RHONE WINES (RED AND WHITE):
Usual names—Chateau Neuf du Pape, Hermitage, Tavel. Drier and harsher than Burgundies. Alcohol 10% to 13%.

SPARKLING WINE:
Usual name—Sparkling Burgundy. Sweeter and richer than other sparkling wines. Alcohol 12% to 14%. Serve thoroughly chilled. Suitable at dessert also.

DESSERT

CHAMPAGNE:
Doux—very sweet. Sec—sweet, delicate, light taste. Alcohol 13% to 14%. Serve thoroughly chilled.

MADEIRA:
Light and delicate with more body than natural wines. Alcohol 18% to 21%. Serve at room temperature.

MALAGA:
Closely resembles sherry, but is much sweeter and without the characteristic nuttiness. Alcohol 18% to 21%. Serve at room temperature.

MUSCATEL:

Rich, fruity flavor, fairly sweet. Alcohol 20%. Serve at room temperature.

SHERRY:

Usual names—Oloroso, and other sweet sherrys. Nutty aromatic flavor, elusively sweet. Alcohol 19% to 21%. Serve at room temperature.

TOKAY (AMBER):

Light and delicate with a very distinctive flavor. Alcohol 15% to 18%. Serve at room temperature.

WHITE BORDEAUX:

Usual names—Haut Sauterne, Sauterne. Distinctive, delicate flavor and bouquet. Always sweet. Alcohol 10% to 20%. Serve at 20° below room temperature.

FRUIT AND NUTS

PORT:

Usual names—Burgundy Port, Oporto, Superior, Tawny. Delicate and distinctive bouquet. Full in body. Rich and sweet. Alcohol 10% to 21%. Serve at room temperature. Mainly red.

ENTIRE MEAL

RED BORDEAUX:

Usual names—Margaux, Ponte Canet, Red Graves, St. Emillon, St. Estephe, St. Julien, many other "Chateau" wines. Body and flavor is light and dry. Alcohol 10% to 12%. Serve at room temperature Also can be served with entree or roast.

Copyright 1934 by
Charles E. Graham & Co.
Newark, N. J.
Made in U. S. A.

Made in the USA
Lexington, KY
15 May 2013